HOLY

Spurgeon on the

SPIRIT

HOLY

Spurgeon on the

SPIRIT

Charles Spurgeon

🆄 *Whitaker House*

SPURGEON ON THE HOLY SPIRIT

ISBN: 0-88368-622-8
Printed in the United States of America
Copyright © 2000 by Whitaker House

Whitaker House
30 Hunt Valley Circle
New Kensington, PA 15068

Library of Congress Cataloging-in-Publication Data

Spurgeon, C. H. (Charles Haddon), 1834–1892.
  Spurgeon on the Holy Spirit / by Charles Haddon Spurgeon.
      p. cm.
  ISBN 0-88368-622-8 (pbk.)
  1. Holy Spirit. I. Title.
  BT121.2 .S677 2000
  231'.3—dc21   00-011929

1 2 3 4 5 6 7 8 9 10 11 12 13 / 08 07 06 05 04 03 02 01 00

Contents

Introduction

Charles Haddon Spurgeon was born on June 19, 1834, at Kelvedon, Essex, England, the firstborn of eight surviving children. His parents were committed Christians, and his father was a preacher. Spurgeon was converted in 1850 at the age of fifteen. He began to help the poor and to hand out tracts; he was known as "The Boy Preacher."

His next six years were eventful. He preached his first sermon at the age of sixteen. At age eighteen, he became the pastor of Waterbeach Baptist Chapel, preaching in a barn. Spurgeon preached over six hundred times before he reached the age of twenty. By 1854, he was well-known and was asked to become the pastor of New Park Street Chapel in London. In 1856, Spurgeon married Susannah Thompson; they had twin sons, both of whom later entered the ministry.

Spurgeon's compelling sermons and lively preaching style drew multitudes of people, and many came to Christ. Soon, the crowds had grown so large that they blocked the narrow streets near the church. Services eventually had to be held in rented halls, and Spurgeon often preached to congregations of more than ten thousand. The Metropolitan Tabernacle was built in 1861 to accommodate the large numbers of people.

Spurgeon published over thirty-five hundred sermons, which were so popular that they sold by the ton. At one point, twenty-five thousand copies of his sermons sold every week. The prime minister of England, members of the royal family, and Florence Nightingale, among others, went to hear him preach. Spurgeon preached to an estimated ten million people throughout his life. Not surprisingly, he is called the "Prince of Preachers."

In addition to his powerful preaching, Spurgeon founded and supported charitable outreaches, including educational institutions. His pastors' college, which is still in existence today, taught nearly nine hundred students in Spurgeon's time. He also founded the famous Stockwell Orphanage.

Charles Spurgeon died in 1892, and his death was mourned by many.

Chapter 1

The Work of the Holy Spirit

Are ye so foolish? having begun in the Spirit,
are ye now made perfect by the flesh?
—Galatians 3:3

Yes, in response to the question in our text, we are this foolish. Folly is bound up not only in the heart of a child, but even in the heart of a child of God; and though the rod may be said to bring folly out of a child (Prov. 22:15), it will take many repetitions of the rod of affliction upon the shoulders of a Christian before that folly is taken out of him.

I suppose we are all of us very sound as a matter of theory upon this point. If any should ask us how we hope to have our salvation worked in us, we would, without the slightest hesitation, state our belief that *"salvation is of the LORD"* (Jonah 2:9) alone, and we would declare that, as the Holy Spirit first of all began our piety in us, we look alone to His might to continue, preserve, and at last perfect the sacred work (Phil. 1:6).

I say we are sound enough on this point as a matter of theory, but we are all of us very heretical and unsound as a matter of practice; sadly, you will not find a Christian who does not have to mourn

9

over his self-righteous tendencies. You will not discover
a believer who has not, at certain periods in his life,
needed to groan because the spirit of self-confidence
has risen in his heart and prevented him from feeling the absolute necessity of the Holy Spirit. This
dependence on self has led him to put his confidence
in the mere strength of nature, the strength of good
intentions, or the strength of strong resolutions, instead of relying upon the might of God the Holy
Spirit alone. This one thing I know, friends, that
while, as a preacher, I can tell you that the Holy
Spirit must work all our works in us, and that without Him we can do nothing, yet as a man, I find myself tempted to deny my own preaching, not in my
words, but to deny them in fact, by endeavoring to
do deeds without looking first to the Holy Spirit.

While I would never be unsound in the teaching
part of it, in that part that concerns the working of it
out, in common with all who love the Lord Jesus, but
who are still subject to the infirmities of flesh and
blood, I have to admit with sorrow that I repeatedly
find myself *"having begun in the Spirit,"* seeking to
be made perfect in the flesh.

Yes, we are as foolish as that; and, beloved, it is
well for us if we have a consciousness that we are
foolish, for when a man is foolish and knows it, there
is the hope that he will one day be wise. To know
one's self to be foolish is to stand upon the doorstep
of the temple of wisdom; to understand the wrong-
ness of any position is halfway toward amending it;
to be quite sure that our self-confidence is a heinous
sin and folly, and an offense toward God, and to have
that thought burned into us by God's Holy Spirit, is
going a great length toward the absolute casting of

our self-confidence away, and the bringing of our souls in practice, as well as in theory, to rely wholly upon the power of God's Holy Spirit.

However, I will leave my text somewhat. Having just in a few words endeavored to explain the meaning of the whole sentence, I intend to dwell only upon the doctrine that, incidentally, the apostle Paul taught. He taught us that we begin in the Spirit—*"Having begun in the Spirit."* I have already illustrated the whole text sufficiently for our understanding if God the Holy Spirit will enlighten us. I will now confine myself to the thought that Christians begin in the Spirit; that the early part of Christianity is of God's Spirit, and of God's Spirit only; while it is equally true that all the way through we must lean upon the same power and depend upon the same strength.

I have selected this text for this reason: we have a very large influx of young believers, month after month, week after week; every week we receive additions to the church in a considerable number. Month after month these hands baptize into a profession of faith in the Lord Jesus many of those who are yet young in the faith of the Gospel.

Now, I am astonished to find those persons who thus come before me so well instructed in the doctrines of grace and so sound in all the truths of the covenant, insomuch that I may think it my boast and glory, in the name of Jesus, that I do not know of any members whom we have received into the church who do not give their full assent and consent to all the doctrines of the Christian religion. Doctrines that others are accustomed to laugh at as being high doctrinal points are those that these new

Christians most readily receive, believe, and rejoice in. I find, however, that the greatest deficiency lies in this point: forgetfulness of the work of the Holy Spirit.

I find them very easily remembering the work of God the Father. They do not deny the great doctrine of election; they can see clearly the great sentence of justification passed by the Father upon the elect through the vicarious sacrifice and perfect righteousness of Jesus. Additionally, they are not backward in understanding the work of Jesus either. They can see how Christ was the Substitute for His people and stood in their place. Nor do they for one moment impugn any doctrine concerning God's Spirit, but they are not clear upon the aforementioned point. They can talk upon the other points better than they can upon those that more particularly concern the blessed work of that all-adorable person of the Godhead, God the Holy Spirit.

I thought, therefore, that I would preach as simply as ever I could upon the work of the Holy Spirit and begin at the beginning. I hope at other times, as God the Holy Spirit will guide me, to enter more fully into the subject of the work of the Spirit from the beginning to the end.

But let me say that it is no use your expecting me to preach a series of sermons. I know a great deal better than that. I don't believe God the Holy Spirit ever intended men to publish three months beforehand lists of sermons that they were going to preach because there always will arise changes in providence, and different states of mind both in the preacher and the hearer, and he will be a very wise

man who has got an *Old Moore's Almanack** correct
enough to let him know what would be the best sort
of sermon to preach three months ahead. He had
better leave it to his God to give him in the same
hour what he will speak, and look for his sermons as
the Israelites looked for the manna, day by day. (See
Exodus 16:14–27.) However, we now begin by endeavoring to narrate the different points of the
Spirit's work in the beginning of salvation.

SALVATION BEGINS WITH THE WORK OF THE HOLY SPIRIT

NOT BY MEANS OF GRACE ALONE

First, let me start by asserting that salvation is
not begun in the soul by the means of grace apart
from the Holy Spirit. No man in the world is at liberty to neglect the means that God has appointed. If
a house is built for prayer, no man must expect a
blessing who neglects to tread its floor. If a pulpit is
erected for the ministry of the Word, no man must
expect (although we do sometimes get more than we
expect) to be saved except by the hearing of the
Word. If the Bible is printed in our own native language, and we can read it, he who neglects the Holy
Scripture and ceases from its study has lost one
great and grand opportunity of being blessed. There
are many means of grace, and let us speak as highly
of them as ever we can. We would be far from depreciating them, for they are of the highest value.

---

* Authored by Francis Moore [1657–1715]. First edition was published in 1697.

Blessed are the people who have them, and happy is the nation that is blessed with the means of grace. But, my friends, no one was ever saved by the means of grace apart from the Holy Spirit.

You may hear the sermons of the man whom God delights to honor; you may select from all your Puritan clergy the writings of the man whom God has blessed with a double portion of His Holy Spirit; you may attend every meeting for prayer; you may turn over the leaves of the blessed Book; but in all this, there is no life for the soul apart from the breath of the divine Spirit. Use these means; we exhort you to use them, and use them diligently, but recollect that in none of these means is there anything that can benefit you unless God the Holy Spirit will own and crown them. These are like the conduit pipes of the marketplace. When the fountainhead flows with water, then they are full, and we derive a blessing from them; but if the stream is blocked, if the fountainhead ceases to give forth its current, then these are wells without water, clouds without rain. You may go to ordinances as an Arab turns to his skin bottle when it is dry, and with your parched lips you may suck the wind and drink the whirlwind, but receive neither comfort, blessing, nor instruction from the means of grace.

NOT THROUGH MINISTERS OR PRIESTS

Nor is the salvation of any sinner begun in him by a minister or a priest. God forgive the man who ever calls himself a priest or allows anyone else to call him that since the days of our Lord Jesus. The other morning at family prayer, I read the case of

King Uzziah, who, because he was the king, thrust himself into the tabernacle of the Lord to take the place of the priests. You remember how the priests opposed him, and said, *"It is not for you, Uzziah, to burn incense to the LORD, but for the priests, the sons of Aaron, who are consecrated to burn incense"* (2 Chron. 26:18 NKJV). Remember how he seized the censer and angrily insisted on burning incense as a priest before the Lord God. While he was still speaking, leprosy appeared on his face, and he went out a leper, as white as snow, from the house of God.

Oh, my friends, it is no small offense against God for any man to call himself a priest. All the saints have a priestly office through Christ Jesus, but when any man asserts the idea that he has a calling that elevates him above his fellowman, and he claims to be a priest among men, he commits a sin before God. Even though it is a sin of ignorance, it is indeed great and grievous and leads to many deadly errors, the guilt of which must lie partly upon the head of the man who gave a basis for those errors by allowing the title to be applied to himself.

Well, there is no man—call him priest if you like, by way of ill courtesy—who can begin the work with us—no, not in the use of the ceremony. The Papist may tell us that grace begins in the heart at the dropping of the water upon the child's brow; but he tells a lie, a lie before God, that does not even have so much as the shadow of truth to justify the liar. There is no power in man, even if he was ordained by one who could most assuredly claim succession from the apostles, even if he was endowed with miraculous gifts, or even if he was the apostle Paul himself. If he asserted that he had in himself the power to convert or the power to regenerate, let him be accursed, for he has denied the truth, and Paul himself would have declared him *"Anathema Maranatha"* (1 Cor. 16:22; *"accursed,"* NKJV) for having departed from the everlasting Gospel, one cardinal point of which is that regeneration is the work of God the Holy Spirit; the new birth is a thing that is from above.

NOT BY SELF-EFFORTS

And, my brethren, it is quite certain that no man ever begins the new birth himself. The work of salvation never started with the efforts of any man. God the Holy Spirit must begin it. Now, the reasons no man ever started the work of grace in his own heart are very apparent: first, because he cannot; second, because he won't. The best reason of all is because he cannot; he is dead. The dead may be made alive, but the dead cannot make themselves alive, for the dead can do nothing. Besides, the new thing to be created as yet has no being. The uncreated cannot create. But you say, "Man can create." Well, if hell can create heaven, then sin can create grace.

What! Will you tell me that fallen human nature, which has come almost to a level with the beasts, is competent to rival God? Can it emulate the divinity in working as great marvels and in imparting as divine a life as even God Himself can give? It cannot. Besides, it is a creation; we are created anew in Christ Jesus (2 Cor. 5:17). Let any man create a fly, and afterward let him create a new heart in himself; until he has done the lesser thing, he cannot do the greater. Besides, no man will. If any man could convert himself, there is no man who would. If any man says that he would, if that is true, he is already converted, for the will to be converted is in great part conversion. The will to love God, the desire to be in unison with Christ, is not to be found in any man who has not already been brought to be reconciled with God through the death of His Son. There may be a false desire, a desire grounded upon a misrepresentation of the truth, but a true desire after true salvation by the true Spirit is a certain indication that the salvation already is there in the germ and in the bud, and needs only time and grace to develop itself. But it is certain that man neither can nor will save himself—being on the one hand utterly impotent and dead, and on the other hand utterly depraved and unwilling, hating the change when he sees it in others, and most of all despising it in himself. Be certain, therefore, that God the Holy Spirit must begin the work since no one else can do so.

What the Holy Spirit Does

And now, my brethren, I must enter into the subject very briefly, by showing what the Holy Spirit does in the beginning. Permit me to say that in describing the work, the true work of salvation in the soul, you must not expect me to exhibit any critical distinction in judgment. We have heard of an assembly of clergymen who once debated whether men repented first or believed first; and after a long discussion, someone wiser than the rest suggested another question, whether in the newborn child if the lungs inflated first, or if the blood circulated first. "Now," said he, "when you will find the answer to the one, you may be able to know the answer to the other."

You will not know which comes first—repenting or believing; they are, very likely, begotten in us at the same moment. We are not able, when we mention these things in order, exactly to declare and testify that these all happen according to the order in which we mention them; but, according to the judgment of men and to my own experience, I seek now to set forth what is the usual way of acting with God the Holy Spirit in the work of salvation.

REGENERATES THE SOUL

The first thing, then, that God the Holy Spirit does in the soul is to regenerate it. We must always learn to distinguish between regeneration and conversion. A man may be converted a great many times in his life, but regenerated only once. Conversion is a thing that is caused by regeneration, but regeneration is the very first act of God the Spirit in the soul. You ask, "Does regeneration come before conviction of sin?" Most certainly; there could be no conviction in the dead sinner. Now, regeneration quickens the sinner and makes him live. He is not competent to have true spiritual conviction worked in him until, first of all, he has received life. It is true that one of the earliest developments of life is conviction of sin, but before any man can see his need of a Savior, he must be a living man. Before he can really, I mean, in a spiritual position, in a saving, effective manner, understand his own deep depravity, he must have eyes with which to see the depravity. He must have ears with which to hear the sentence of the law. He must have been quickened and made alive; otherwise, he could not be capable of feeling, seeing, or discerning at all.

I believe, then, the first thing the Spirit does is this: he finds the sinner dead in sin, just where Adam left him; he breathes into him a divine influence. The sinner knows nothing about how it is done, nor do any of us understand it. As the Scripture says,

> *The wind bloweth where it listeth, and thou hearest the sound thereof, but canst not tell whence it cometh, and whither it goeth: so is every one that is born of the Spirit.* (John 3:8)

Now, none of us can tell how the Holy Spirit works in men. I do not doubt there have been some who have sat in these pews, and in the middle of a sermon or in prayer or singing—they did not understand how it happened—and the Spirit of God was in their hearts. He had entered their souls, and they were no longer dead in sin, no longer without thought, without hope, without spiritual capacity, but they had begun to live. And I believe this work of regeneration, when it is done effectively—and God the Spirit would not do it without doing it effectively—is done mysteriously, often suddenly, and it is done in various ways, but still it has always this mark about it: that the man, although he may not understand how it is done, feels that something is done. The what, the how, he does not know, but he knows that something is done, and he now begins to think thoughts he never thought before. He begins to feel as he never felt before. He is brought into a new state; there is a change worked in him—as if a dead post standing in the street were suddenly to find itself possessed of a soul and to hear the sound of the passing carriages, to listen to the words of the passengers. There is something quite new about it.

The fact is, the man does have a spirit; he never had one before; he was nothing but a body and a soul; but now, God has breathed into him the third great principle, the new life, the Spirit, and he has become a spiritual man. Now, he is not only capable of mental exercise, but also of spiritual exercise.

Having a soul, he could repent, and he could believe. As a mere mental exercise, he could think thoughts of God and have some desires after Him, but he could not have one spiritual thought or one spiritual wish or desire, for he had no powers that could elicit these things; yet now, in regeneration, he has got something given to him, and being given, you soon see its effects. The man begins to feel that he is a sinner. Why did he not feel that before? Ah, my brethren, he could not. He was not in a state to feel; he was a dead sinner, and though he used to tell you, and tell God, by way of a compliment, that he was a sinner, he did not know anything about it. He said he was a sinner, but he talked about being a sinner just as the blind man talks about the stars that he has never seen, as he talks about the light, the existence of which he would not know unless he were told of it; but now it is a deep reality. You may laugh at him, you who have not been regenerated, but now he has got something that really puts him beyond your laughter. He begins to feel the exceeding weight and evil of transgression; his heart trembles, his very flesh quivers—in some cases the whole frame is affected. The man is sick by day and night. His flesh creeps on his bones for fear. He cannot eat, and his appetite fails him. He cannot bear the sound of melody and mirth. All his fleshly spirits are dried up. He cannot rejoice. He is unhappy, miserable, downcast, distressed, and, in some cases, almost ready to go mad. Although in the majority of cases, it takes a lighter phase, and there are the gentle whispers of the Spirit, even then, the pangs and pains caused by regeneration, while the new life reveals the sin and evil of the past condition of the man, are things that are not to be well described or mentioned without tears. This is all the work of the Spirit.

REVEALS MAN'S INABILITY TO SAVE HIMSELF

And having brought the soul thus far, the next thing the Holy Spirit does is to teach the soul that it is utterly incapable of saving itself. The man knew that before, perhaps, if he sat under a Gospel ministry, but he only heard it with his ears and understood it with his mind. Now, it has become part of his very life. He feels it; it has entered into his soul, and he knows it to be true. Once he thought he would be good, and thought that would save him. The Holy Spirit just knocks the brains out of that thought. "Then," he says, "I will try ceremonies and see whether I cannot gain merit in that way." God the Holy Spirit shoots the arrow right through the heart of that thought, and it falls dead before him. He cannot bear the sight of the carcass, so that, like Abraham said of Sarah, he exclaims, "Bury the dead out of my sight." (See Genesis 23:2–11.) Though once he loved it dearly, now he hates the sight thereof. He thought once that he could believe; he had an Arminian[*] notion in his head, that he could believe when he liked and repent when he liked. Now, God the Spirit has brought him to such a condition that he says, "I can do nothing." He begins to discover his own death, now that he is made alive. He did not know anything about it before. He now finds that he has no hand of faith to lift, though the minister tells him to do it. He now discovers, when he is bidden to pray, that he wants to, but he cannot pray. He now finds that he is powerless, and he dies in the hand of God like clay in the hand of the potter, and is made to cry out, "O Lord, my God, unless You save me, I am damned for all eternity, for I cannot lift a finger in this matter until first of all You give me strength." And if you urge him to do anything, he longs to be doing, but he is so afraid that it would only be fleshly doings, and not the doings of the Spirit, that he meditates, stops, and waits, until he groans and cries. Feeling that these groans and cries are the real work of the Spirit, and prove that he has spiritual life, he then begins in earnest to look to Jesus Christ, the Savior. But mark, all these things are caused by the Spirit, and none of them can ever be produced in the soul of any man or woman, apart from the divine influence of God the Holy Spirit.

APPLIES THE BLOOD

This being done, the soul, weaned from all confidence, despairing, and brought to its last standing

---

[*] Jacobus Arminius (1560–1609), a Dutch theologian, opposed strict Calvinist teachings about predestination and believed in the possibility of salvation for all.

place, lies prostrate on the ground. The rope is tied about its neck, and the ashes and sackcloth are on its head. God the Holy Spirit next applies the blood of Jesus to the soul, gives it the grace of faith whereby it lays hold of Jesus, and gives it an anointing of holy consolation and unction of assurance, whereby, casting itself wholly on the blood and righteousness of Jesus, it receives joy, knows itself to be saved, and rejoices in pardon.

But note, that is the work of the Spirit. Some preachers will tell their people, "Believe; only believe." Yes, it is right that they should tell them so, but they should remember it is also right to tell them that even this must be the work of the Spirit; for although we say, "Only believe," that is the greatest *only* in the world. What some men say is so easy is just what those who want to believe find to be the hardest thing in all the world. It is simple enough for a man who has the Spirit in him to believe, when he has the written Word before him and the witness of the Spirit in him; that is easy enough. But for the poor, tried sinner, who cannot see anything in the Word of God but thunder and threatening—for him to believe—ah, my brethren, it is not such a little matter as some make it to be. The fullness of the power of God's Spirit is needed to bring any man to such faith as that.

Avails the Soul of Blessings

When the sinner has thus believed, then the Holy Spirit brings all the precious things to him. There is the blood of Jesus. That can never save my soul, unless God the Spirit takes the blood and sprinkles it upon my conscience. There is the perfect, spotless righteousness of Jesus. It is a robe that will fit me and adorn me from head to foot, but it is no use to me until I have put it on, and I cannot put it on myself. God the Holy Spirit must put the robe of Jesus' righteousness on me. There is the covenant of adoption, whereby God gives me the privileges of a son, but I cannot rejoice in my adoption until I receive *"the Spirit of adoption, whereby* [I] *cry, Abba, Father"* (Rom. 8:15). So, beloved, you see—I might enlarge on these truths, but my time fails me—you see that every point that is brought out in the experience of the newborn Christian, every point in that part of salvation that we may call its beginning in the soul, has to do with God the Holy Spirit.

There is no step that can be taken without Him. There is nothing that can be accomplished right without Him. Even though you had the best of means, the rightest of ceremonies, the most orthodox of truths, and though you exercised your minds upon all these things, and though the blood of Jesus Christ were shed for you, and God Himself had ordained you from before the foundation of the world to be saved, yet still there must be that one link always inserted in the golden chain of the plan of salvation; for without that it would all be incomplete. You must be quickened by the Spirit; you must be called out of darkness into light; you must be made *"a new creature"* (2 Cor. 5:17) in Christ Jesus.

EXCUSES FALL SHORT

Now, I wonder how many of you know anything about this. That is the practical part of it. Now, my friend, do you understand this? Perhaps you are exceedingly wise, and you turn on your heel with a sneer. You say, "Supernaturalism in one of its phases—these Methodists are always talking about supernatural things." You are very wise, no doubt, but it seems to me that Nicodemus of old had gotten as far as you, and you have gone no further than he. He asked, *"How can a man be born when he is old?"* (John 3:4). And though every Sunday school child has had a smile at the expense of Nicodemus's ignorance, you are not wiser. And yet you are a Rabbi, sir, and you would teach us, would you? (See verse 10.) You would teach us about these things, and yet you sneer about supernaturalism. Well, the day may come—I pray it may come to you before the day of your death and your doom—when the Christ of the supernaturalists will be the only Christ for you; when you will come into the floods of death, where you will need something more than nature, then you will be crying for a work that is supernatural within your heart. It may be that then, when you first of all awake to know that your wisdom was but one of the methods of madness, you may perhaps have to cry in vain, having for your only answer, "I called, and you refused; I stretched out my hands, and no man regarded. I also will mock at your calamity and laugh when your fear comes." (See Proverbs 1:24, 26.)

I hear another of you say, "Well, sir, I know nothing of this work of God the Holy Spirit in my heart. I am just as good as other people. I never make a profession of religion; it is very rarely that I go into a place of worship at all, but I am as good as the saints, any of them. Look at some of them—very fine fellows certainly."

Stop, now. Religion is a thing between you and your Maker, and you have nothing to do with those very fine fellows you have spoken of. Suppose I make a confession that a large number of those who are called saints deserve a great deal more to be called sinners double-dyed, and then whitewashed. Suppose I make a confession of that. What has that to do with you? Your religion must be for yourself, and it must be between you and your God. If all the world were hypocrites, that would not exonerate you before your God. When you came before the Master, if you were still at enmity with Him, could you venture to plead such an excuse as this: "All the world was full of hypocrites"? "Well," He would say, "what did that have to do with you? So much the more why you should have been an honest man. If you say the church was drifting away into quicksand, through the evil conduct and folly of the members thereof, so much the more why you should have helped to make it sound, if you thought you could have done so."

Another cries, "Well, I do not see that I need it. I am as moral a man as I can be. I never break the Sabbath. I am one of the most conscientious of Christians. I always go to church twice on Sunday. I listen to a thoroughly evangelical minister, and you would not find fault with him." Perhaps another says, "I go to a Baptist chapel. I am always found there, and I am scrupulously correct in my conduct. I am a good father, a good husband. I do not know that any man can find fault with me in business." Well, certainly, that is very good, and if you will be so good tomorrow morning as to go into Saint Paul's and wash one of those statues until you make it alive, then you will be saved by your morality; but since you, even you, are *dead in trespasses and sins"* (Eph. 2:1), without the Spirit you may wash yourself ever so clean, but you cannot wash life into you any more than those statues, by all your washing, could be made to walk or think or breathe. You must be quickened by the Holy Spirit, for you are dead in trespasses and sins.

Yes, my lovely maiden, you who are everything excellent; you who are not to be blamed in anything; you who are affectionate, tender, kind, and dutiful. Your very life seems to be so pure that all who see you think that you are an angel. Even you, unless you are born again, cannot see the kingdom of God. The golden gate of heaven must grind upon its hinges with a doleful sound and shut you out forever, unless you are the subject of a divine change, for this requirement permits no exception.

And, you, vilest of the vile, you who have wandered farthest from the paths of righteousness, *"ye must be born again"* (John 3:7). You must be quickened by a divine life, and it is comforting for you to remember that the very same power that can awaken the moral man, that can save the righteous and honest man, is able to work in you, is able to change you. This power can turn the lion into a lamb, and the raven into a dove.

Oh, my readers, ask yourselves, are you the subjects of this change? And if you are, rejoice with joy unspeakable, for happy is that mother's child, and full of glory, who can say, "I am born of God." Blessed is that man. God and the holy angels call him blessed who has received the quickening of the Spirit and is born of God. For him there may be many troubles, but there is *"a far more exceeding and eternal weight of glory"* (2 Cor. 4:17) to counterbalance all his woe; for him there may be wars and fightings, but let him tarry. There are trumpets of victory, there are better wreaths than the laurels of conquerors, there is a crown of immortal glory, there is bliss unfading, there is acceptance in the breast of God, and perpetual fellowship with Jehovah. But, oh, if you are not born again, I can but tremble for you and lift my heart in prayer to God, and pray for you, that He may now by His divine Spirit make you alive, show you your need of Him, and then direct you to the cross of Jesus.

But if you know your need of a Savior, if you are conscious of your death in sin, listen to the Gospel. The Lord Jesus Christ died for you. Do you know yourself to be guilty, not as the hypocrite pretends to know it, but do you know it consciously, sensitively? Do you weep over it? Do you lament it? Do you feel that you cannot save yourself? Are you sick of all fleshly ways of saving? Can you say right now, "Unless God reaches out His hand of mercy, I know I deserve to be lost forever, and I am"? Then, as the Lord my God lives, before whom I stand, my Master bought you with His blood, and those whom He bought with His blood, He will have; from the fangs of the lion and the jaws of the bear will He pluck them. He will save you, for you are a part of His bloody purchase; He has taken your sins upon His head; He suffered in your place. He has been punished for you; you will not die; "your sins, which are many, are all forgiven." (See Luke 7:47.) I am the Master's glad herald to tell you what His Word tells you also, that you may rejoice in the fullness of faith, for *"Christ Jesus came into the world to save sinners"* (1 Tim. 1:15), and *"this is a faithful saying, and worthy of all acceptation"* (v. 15). May the Lord now be pleased to add His blessing for Jesus' sake.

Chapter 2

The Necessity of the Work of the Spirit

I will put My Spirit within you.
—Ezekiel 36:27 NKJV

T he miracles of Christ are remarkable, in part, because none of them were unnecessary. The pretended miracles of Muhammad, and of the Church of Rome, even if they had been miracles, would have been acts of folly. Suppose that St. Denis* *had* walked with his head in his hand after it had been cut off; what practical purpose would have been served by that? He would certainly have been quite as well off in his grave, for any practical good he could have conferred on men.

The miracles of Christ were never unnecessary. They were not capricious demonstrations of power. It is true that they were displays of power, but all of them have a practical end. The same thing may be said of the promises of God. Not one promise in the Scripture may be regarded as a mere whim of grace.

---

* Italian missionary to Paris, France. He was beheaded circa A.D. 258, and his body was thrown into the Seine River. A legend that came out of his martyrdom was that he carried his severed head some distance beyond his execution site.

As every miracle was necessary, absolutely necessary, so is every promise that is given in the Word of God. Hence, from the text that is before us, may I draw, and I think I may very conclusively, the argument that, if God in His covenant made with His people has promised to put His Spirit within them, it must be absolutely necessary that this promise should have been made, and it must be absolutely necessary also to our salvation that every one of us should receive the Spirit of God.

This topic will be the subject of my discourse. I will not hope to make it very interesting, except to those who are anxiously longing to know the way of salvation.

We start, then, by laying down this proposition: that the work of the Holy Spirit is absolutely necessary to us, if we would be saved.

CONSIDER MAN'S NATURE

In endeavoring to prove our need of the Holy Spirit, I would first of all state that the need is very obvious if we remember what man is by nature. Some say that man may through his own efforts attain salvation—that if he hears the Word, it is in his power to receive it, to believe it, and to have a saving change worked in him by it.

To this we reply, You do not know what man is by nature; otherwise, you would never have ventured to make such an assertion. Holy Scripture tells us that man by nature is *"dead in trespasses and sins"* (Eph. 2:1). It does not say that he is sick; that he is faint; that he has grown callous, hardened, and seared, but it says he is absolutely dead. Whatever the term *death* means in connection with the body, it also means in connection with man's soul, viewing it in its relation to spiritual things. When the body is dead, it is powerless. It is unable to do anything for itself. And when the soul of man is dead, in a spiritual sense, it must be, if there is any meaning in the comparison, utterly and entirely powerless and unable to do anything of itself or for itself. When you see dead men raising themselves from their graves, unwinding their own shrouds, opening their own coffin lids, and walking down the streets alive and animate, as the result of their own powers, then perhaps you will believe that souls that are dead in sin may turn to God, may recreate their own natures, and may make themselves heirs of heaven, though before they were heirs of wrath. But mark, not until then.

The substance of the Gospel is that man is dead in sin and that divine life is God's gift. You must go contrary to the whole meaning before you can suppose that a man is brought to know and love Christ apart from the work of the Holy Spirit.

The Spirit finds men as destitute of spiritual life as Ezekiel's dry bones. He brings bone to bone, fits the skeleton together, and then comes from the four winds and breathes into the slain, and they live and stand upon their feet, an exceeding great army, and worship God. (See Ezekiel 37:4–10.) But apart from that, apart from the vivifying influence of the Spirit of God, men's souls must lie in the valley of dry bones, dead, and dead forever.

Scripture not only tells us that man is dead in sin, but also something worse than this, namely, that he is utterly and entirely averse to everything that is good and right. *"The carnal mind is enmity against God: for it is not subject to the law of God, neither indeed can be"* (Rom. 8:7).

Look all through Scripture, and you will find continually that the will of man is described as being contrary to the things of God. What did Christ say to those who imagined that men would come to God without divine influence? He said, first, *"No one can come to Me unless the Father who sent Me draws him"* (John 6:44 NKJV), but He said something even stronger, *"You are not willing to come to Me that you may have life"* (John 5:40 NKJV).

No one will come. Here lies the deadly mischief; man is not only powerless to do good, but also powerful enough to do what is wrong, and his will is desperately set against everything that is right. Men will not come. They will never come of themselves. You cannot induce them to come. You cannot force them to come by all your clamorous warnings, nor can you entice them to come by all your gentle invitations. They will not come to Christ that they may have life. Until the Spirit draws them, neither will they come, nor can they come.

Hence, then, from the fact that man's nature is hostile to the divine Spirit, that he hates grace, that he despises the way in which grace is brought to him, that it is contrary to his own proud nature to stoop to receive salvation by the deeds of another, it is necessary that the Spirit of God should operate to change the will, to correct the bias of the heart, to set man on a right track, and then give him strength to run on it. Oh, if you read men and understand them, you cannot help being sound on the point of the necessity of the Holy Spirit's work.

It has been well said by a noted writer that he never knew a man who believed any great theological error, who did not also support a doctrine that diminished the depravity of man. It is true that the Arminian believes that man is fallen, but then he says that man has the power of his free will left, and that he can raise himself. He diminishes the desperate character of the fall of man.

On the other hand, the Antinomian says that man cannot do anything. But he also says that man is not at all responsible and is not bound to do it. It is not his duty to believe or to repent. Thus, you see, he also diminishes the sinfulness of man and does not have the right view of the Fall.

But once you understand the correct view, that man is utterly fallen, powerless, guilty, defiled, lost, condemned, then you must be sound on all points of the great Gospel of Jesus Christ. Once you believe man to be what Scripture says he is—once you believe that his heart is depraved, his affections perverted, his understanding darkened, his will perverse—you must hold that if such a wretch as that is saved, it must be as a result of the work of the Spirit of God, and of the Spirit of God alone.

CONSIDER THE MEANS OF SALVATION

Salvation must be the work of the Spirit in us, because the means used in salvation are of themselves inadequate to accomplish the work. And what are the means of salvation?

PREACHING

First and foremost stands the preaching of the Word of God. More men are brought to Christ by preaching than by anything else, for it is God's chief and first instrument. The Word is the *"sword of the Spirit"* (Eph. 6:17), *"living and powerful, and sharper than any two-edged sword, piercing even to the division of soul and spirit, and of joints and marrow"* (Heb. 4:12 NKJV). *"It pleased God by the foolishness of preaching to save them that believe"* (1 Cor. 1:21).

But what is there in preaching, by which souls are saved, that looks as if it would be the means of saving souls? I could point you to various churches and chapels into which you might step, and say, "Here is an educated minister; indeed, he is a man who would instruct and enlighten the intellect." You sit down and say, "Well, if God means to work a great work, he will use a learned man like this."

But do you know any learned men who are used as the means of bringing souls to Christ, to any great degree? Go around your churches, if you please, and look at them, and then answer the question. Do you know any great men—men great in learning and wisdom—who have become spiritual fathers in our Israel? Is it not a fact that stares us in the face, that our fashionable preachers, our eloquent preachers, our learned preachers, are nearly useless for the winning of souls to Christ?

And where are souls born to God? Why, in the house around which the jeers and the scoffing and the sneers of the world have long gathered. Sinners are converted under the man whose eloquence is rough and homely, the one who has nothing to commend him to his fellowmen, who daily has to fall on his knees and confess his own folly. When the world speaks worst of him, he feels that he deserves it all, since he is nothing but an earthen vessel in which

God is pleased to put His heavenly treasure (2 Cor. 4:7). I will dare to say that, in every age of the world, the most despised ministry has been the most useful. Today, I could show you poor Primitive Methodist preachers who can scarcely speak correct English, who have been the fathers of more souls, and who have brought to Christ more, than any one bishop on the bench. Why, the Lord has always been pleased to make it so. He will clothe the weak and the foolish with power, but He will not clothe with power those who, if good were done, might be led to ascribe the excellence of the power to their learning, their eloquence, or their position. Like the apostle Paul, it is every minister's business to glory in his infirmities (2 Cor. 12:9).

The world says, "Pshaw, on your oratory! It is rough, rude, and eccentric." Yet, even so, we are content, for God blesses it. Then so much the better that it has infirmities in it, for now it will be plainly seen that it is not of man or by man, but the work of God, and of God alone.

It is said that once upon a time a man was exceedingly curious to see the sword with which a mighty hero had fought some desperate battles. Casting his eye along the blade, he said, "Well, I don't see much in this sword."

"No," said the hero, "but you have not examined the arm that wields it."

And so when men come to hear a successful minister, they are apt to say, "I do not see anything in him." No, but you have not examined the eternal arm that reaps its harvest with this sword of the Spirit. If you had looked at the jawbone of the ass in Samson's hand (see Judges 15:15–17), you would have said, "What! You cannot accomplish anything with this! Bring out some polished blade; bring forth the Damascus steel!"

No, for God would have all the glory; therefore, not with polished steel, but with a jawbone, Samson won the victory. So it is with ministers. Usually, God has blessed the weakest to do the most good. Does it not follow from this observation that it must be the work of the Spirit? If there is nothing in the instrument that can lead to the ends, is it not the work of the Spirit when the thing is accomplished?

Let me put it to you this way. Under the ministry, dead souls are quickened, sinners are made to repent, the vilest of sinners are made holy, and men who came determined not to believe are compelled to believe. Now, who does this? If you say the ministry does it, then I say farewell to your reason, because there is nothing in the successful ministry that would support your position. It must be that the Spirit works in man through the ministry or else such deeds would never be accomplished. You might as well expect to raise the dead by whispering in their ears, as hope to save souls by preaching to them, if it were not for the agency of the Spirit.

Melanchthon went out to preach, you know, without the Spirit of the Lord, and he thought he would convert all the people, but he found out at last that old Adam was too strong for young Melanchthon. He had to go back and ask for the help of the Holy Spirit before he ever saw a soul saved.

I say, the fact that the ministry is blessed proves, since there is nothing in the ministry, that salvation must be the work of a Higher Power.

BAPTISM AND THE LORD'S SUPPER

Other means, however, are used to bless men's souls. For instance, the two ordinances of baptism and the Lord's Supper are a rich means of grace. But let me ask you, is there anything in baptism that can possibly bless anybody? Can immersion in water have the slightest tendency to be blessed to the soul? And then with regard to the eating of bread and the drinking of wine at the Lord's Supper, can it by any means be conceived by any rational man that there is anything in the mere piece of bread that we eat, or in the wine that we drink? And yet, undoubtedly, the grace of God does go with both ordinances for the confirming of the faith of those who receive them, and even for the conversion of those who look upon the ceremonies. There must be something, then, beyond the outward ceremony; there must, in fact, be the Spirit of God, witnessing through the water, witnessing through the wine, witnessing through the bread, or otherwise none of these things could be the means of grace to our souls. They could not edify; they could not help us to commune with Christ; they could not tend to the conviction of sinners or to the establishment of saints. There must, then, from these facts, be a higher, unseen, mysterious influence—the influence of the divine Spirit of God.

CONSIDER THE WORKS OF GOD THE FATHER AND GOD THE SON

Let me again remind you, in the third place, that the absolute necessity of the work of the Holy Spirit in the heart may be clearly seen in that all that has been done by God the Father, and all that has been done by God the Son, must be ineffectual to us unless the Spirit reveals these things to our souls.

We believe, in the first place, that God the Father elects His people. From *"before the foundation of the world"* (Eph. 1:4), He has chosen us to Himself, but let me ask you: what effect does the doctrine of election have upon any man until the Spirit of God enters into him? How do I know whether God has chosen me from *"before the foundation of the world"*? How can I possibly know? Can I climb to heaven and read the roll? Is it possible for me to force my way through the thick mists that hide eternity, open the seven seals of the Book (Rev. 5:1), and read my name recorded there?

Ah, no! Election is a dead letter both in my consciousness and in any effect that it can produce upon me, until the Spirit of God calls me *"out of darkness into His marvelous light"* (1 Pet. 2:9 NKJV). And then, through my calling, I see my election, and, knowing myself to be called of God, I know myself to have been chosen of God from *"before the foundation of the world."*

It is a precious thing—that doctrine of election—to a child of God. But what makes it precious? Nothing but the influence of the Spirit. Until the Spirit opens the eye to read, until the Spirit imparts the mystical secret, no heart can know its election. No angel ever revealed to any man that he was chosen of God, but the Spirit does it. He, by His divine workings, bears an infallible witness with our spirits that we are born of God (Rom. 8:16). Then we are enabled to "read our title clear to mansions in the skies."

Look, again, at the covenant of grace. We know that there was a covenant made with the Lord Jesus Christ by His Father from before the foundation of the world, and that, in this covenant, the persons of all His people were given to Him and were secured. But of what use, or of what avail, is the covenant to us, until the Holy Spirit brings the blessings of the covenant to us? The covenant is, as it were, a holy tree, laden with fruit. If the Spirit does not shake that tree and make the fruit fall from it so that it comes within our reach, how can we receive it?

Bring any sinner here and tell him that there is a covenant of grace. Of what advantage is that knowledge to him? "Ah," he says, "I may not be included in it. My name may not be recorded there. I may not be chosen in Christ." But let the Spirit of God dwell in his heart richly, by the faith and the love that is in Christ Jesus, and that man sees the covenant, ordered in all things and sure, and he cries with David, *"This is all my salvation, and all my desire"* (2 Sam. 23:5).

Take, again, the redemption of Christ. We know that Christ stood in the room, place, and stead of all His people, and that all those who will appear in heaven will appear there as an act of justice as well as of grace, seeing that Christ was punished in their stead, and that it would be unjust if God punished them, seeing that He had punished Christ for them. We believe that since Christ paid all their debts, they have a right to their freedom in Christ—that since Christ covered them with His righteousness, they are entitled to eternal life as much as if they had themselves been perfectly holy. But of what avail is this to me, until the Spirit takes of the things of Christ and shows them to me?

What is Christ's blood to any of you until you have received the Spirit of grace? You have heard the minister preach about the blood of Christ a thousand times, but you passed by; it was nothing to you that Jesus died. You know that He atoned for sins that were not His own, but you regarded this knowledge only as a tale, perhaps, even an idle tale. But when the Spirit of God led you to the Cross, opened your eyes, and enabled you to see Christ crucified, ah, then, there was something in the blood indeed. When His hand dipped the hyssop in the blood, and when it applied that blood to your spirit, then there was a joy and peace in believing, such as you had never known before. But, my friend, Christ's dying is nothing to you unless you have a living Spirit within you. Christ brings you no advantage—saving, personal, and lasting—unless the Spirit of God has baptized you in the fountain filled with His blood and washed you from head to foot therein.

I mention only these few out of the many blessings of the covenant just to prove that they are, none of them, of any use to us, unless the Holy Spirit gives them to us. There hang the blessings on the nail—on the nail, Christ Jesus; but we are short of stature. We cannot reach them. The Spirit of God takes them down and gives them to us, and there they are; they are ours. It is like the manna in the skies, far out of mortal reach; but the Spirit of God opens the windows of heaven, brings down the bread, puts it to our lips, and enables us to eat. Christ's blood and righteousness are like wine stored in the wine vat, but we cannot get to them. The Holy Spirit dips our containers into this precious wine, and then we drink. But without the Spirit, we would die and perish, even though the Father elected and the Son redeemed, as though the Father never had elected, and as though the Son never had bought us with His blood. The Spirit is absolutely necessary. Without Him, neither the works of the Father nor of the Son are of any avail to us.

CONSIDER THE EXPERIENCES OF CHRISTIANS

This brings us to another point. The experience of the true Christian is a reality, but it can never be known and felt without the Spirit of God. For what is the experience of the Christian? Let me give just a brief picture of some of its scenes.

RECOGNIZING HIS LOST STATE

A person comes into church one morning. He is one of the most reputable men in London. He has never committed any outward vice; he has never been dishonest. He is known as a staunch, upright tradesman. Now, to his astonishment, he is informed that he is a condemned, lost sinner, and just as surely lost as the thief who died for his crimes upon the cross.

Do you think that man will believe it? Suppose, however, that he does believe it, simply because he reads it in the Bible. Do you think he will ever be made to feel it? I know you say, "Impossible!" Some of you, even now, perhaps, are saying, "Well, I never would!" Can you imagine that honorable, upright businessman saying, "God, be merciful to me, a sinner"—while he stands side by side with the harlot and the swearer? Can you imagine him feeling in his own heart as if he was as guilty as they, and using the same prayer and saying, "Lord, save, or I perish"?

You cannot conceive it, can you? It is contrary to nature that a man who has been so good as he should put himself down among the chief of sinners. But that will be done before he will be saved; he must feel that guilty before he can enter heaven. Now, I ask, who can bring him to such a leveling experience as that, except for the Spirit of God? You know very well that his proud nature will not stoop to it. We are all aristocrats in our own righteousness; we do not like to bend down and come among common sinners. If we are brought there, it must be the Spirit of God who casts us to the ground.

Why, I know that if anyone had told me that I would ever cry to God for mercy and confess that I had been the vilest of the vile, I would have laughed in his face. I would have said, "Why, I have not done anything particularly wrong. I have not hurt anybody." And yet I know this very day that I can take my place on the lowest form, and if I can get inside heaven, I will feel happy to sit among the chief of sinners and praise the almighty love that has saved even me from my sins.

Now, what works this humiliation of heart? Grace. It is contrary to nature for an honest and an upright man in the eyes of the world to consider himself to be a lost sinner. It must be the Holy Spirit's work, or else it never will be done.

RELYING ON CHRIST'S RIGHTEOUSNESS

After a man has been brought to this place, can you conceive that man at last conscience-stricken and led to believe that his past life deserves the wrath of God? His first thought would be, "Well, now, I will live better than I have ever lived." He would say, "Now I will try to play the hermit, pinch myself here and there, deny myself, and do penance; in that way, by paying attention to the outward ceremonies of religion, together with a high moral character, I do not doubt that I will blot out whatever slurs and stains there have been against me."

Can you imagine that man feeling that, if he ever gets to heaven, he will have to get there through the righteousness of another? "Through the righteousness of another?" he asks. "I don't want to be rewarded for what another man does—not I. If I go there, I will go there and take my chance. I will go there through what I do myself. Tell me something to do, and I will do it. I will be proud to do it, however humiliating it may be, so that I may at last win the love and esteem of God."

Now, can you conceive such a man as that brought to feel that he can do nothing—that, as good as he thinks himself to be, he cannot do anything whatsoever to merit God's love and favor? Do you think he will understand that, if he goes to heaven, he must go on the merits of what Christ did? Just the same as the drunkard must go there through the sacrifice of Christ, so this moral man must enter into life having nothing about him but Christ's perfect righteousness, and having been washed in the blood of Jesus. We say that this is so contrary to human nature, so diametrically opposed to all the instincts of our poor fallen humanity, that nothing but the Spirit of God can ever bring a man to strip himself of all self-righteousness, and of all reliance on his own strength, and compel him to rest and lean simply and wholly upon Jesus Christ the Savior.

DEPENDING ON GOD DURING TRIALS

These two examples would be sufficient to prove the necessity of the Holy Spirit to make a man a Christian. But now let me describe a Christian as he is after his conversion. Trouble comes, storms of trouble, and he looks the tempest in the face and says, "I know that all things work together for my good." (See Romans 8:28.) His children die, the partner of his bosom is carried to the grave, and he says, "The Lord gave and the Lord has taken away; blessed be the name of the Lord." (See Job 1:21.) His farm fails, his crop is blighted, his business prospects are clouded, all his wealth seems to vanish, and he is left in poverty. He says,

> *Although the fig tree shall not blossom, neither shall fruit be in the vines; the labour of the olive shall fail, and the fields shall yield no meat; the flock shall be cut off from the fold, and there shall be no herd in the stalls: yet I will rejoice in the LORD, I will joy in the God of my salvation.* (Hab. 3:17–18)

Next, you see him laid upon a sick bed himself, and when he is there, he says, *"It is good for me that I have been afflicted; that I might learn thy statutes"* (Ps. 119:71). You see him approaching at last the dark valley of the shadow of death, and you hear him cry, *"Yea, though I walk through the valley of the shadow of death, I will fear no evil: for thou art with me; thy rod and thy staff they comfort me"* (Ps. 23:4).

I ask you, what makes this man calm in the midst of all these varied trials and personal troubles, if it is not the Spirit of God? Oh, you who doubt the influence of the Spirit, produce the same results without the Spirit. Go and live as Christians live, and die as Christians die. If you can show the same calm resignation, the same quiet joy, and the same firm belief that adverse things will, nevertheless, work together for good, then we may be, perhaps, at liberty to concede the point, but not until then. The high and noble experience of a Christian in times of trials and suffering proves that there must be the operation of the Spirit of God.

DELIGHTING IN GOD

But look at the Christian, too, in his joyous moments. He is rich. God has given him all his heart's desire on earth. Look at him. He says, "I do not value these things at all, except as they are the gifts of God. I hold to them loosely. Notwithstanding this house and home, and all these comforts, I am willing to depart and *'be with Christ; which is far better'* (Phil. 1:23). It is true that I lack nothing here on earth, but still, I feel that to die would be gain to me (v. 21), even though I would leave all these things behind." He holds earth loosely; he does not grasp it with a tight hand, but looks upon it all as dust—a thing that is to pass away. He takes but little pleasure therein, saying, "I've no abiding city here. I seek a city out of sight."

Mark that man. He has plenty of room for pleasures in this world, but he drinks out of a higher cistern. His pleasure springs from things unseen. His happiest moments are when he can shut all these good things out and come to God as a poor guilty sinner. He delights in coming to Christ and entering into fellowship with Him, rising into nearness of access and confidence, and boldly approaching the throne of heavenly grace.

Now, what is it that keeps a man who has all these mercies from setting his heart upon the earth? It is a wonder, indeed, that a man who has gold and silver, flocks and herds, would not make these his god, but that he would still say,

> There's nothing round this spacious earth
> That suits my large desire;
> To boundless joy and solid mirth
> My nobler thoughts aspire.

"These are not my treasure; my treasure is in heaven, and in heaven only." What can do this? No mere moral virtue. No Stoic doctrine ever brought a man to such a place as this. No, it must be the work of the Spirit, and the work of the Spirit alone, that can lead a man to live in heaven, while there is a temptation for him to live on earth.

I do not wonder that a poor man looks forward to heaven; he has nothing to look upon on earth. When there is a thorn in the nest, I do not wonder that the lark flies up, for there is no rest for him below. When you are beaten and chafed by trouble, no wonder you say,

> Jerusalem! my happy home!
> Name ever dear to me;
> When will my labors have an end,
> In joy, and peace, and thee?

But the greatest wonder is that, if you line the Christian's nest ever so softly, if you give him all the mercies of this life, you still cannot keep him from saying,

> To Jesus, the crown of my hope,
> My soul is in haste to be gone;
> Oh, bear me, ye cherubim, up,
> And waft me away to His throne.

Consider the Actions of a Christian

And now, last of all, the actions, the acceptable acts, of the Christian's life, cannot be performed without the Spirit; hence, again, we need the Spirit of God.

Repentance

The first act of the Christian's life is repentance. Have you ever tried to repent? If so, if you tried without the Spirit of God, you know that to urge a man to repent without the promise of the Spirit to help him, is to urge him to do the impossible. A rock might as soon weep, and a desert might as soon blossom, as a sinner repent of his own accord. If God should offer heaven to man, simply upon the terms of repentance of sin, heaven would be as impossible to gain as it is by good works, for a man can no more repent by himself than he can perfectly keep God's law.

Repentance involves the very principle of perfect obedience to the law of God. It seems to me that in repentance there is the whole law solidified and condensed; and if a man can repent by himself, then there is no need of a Savior; he may as well try to

47

reach heaven by climbing up the steep sides of Mount Sinai itself.

FAITH

Faith is the next act in the divine life. Perhaps you think faith is very easy to exercise, but if you are ever brought to feel the burden of sin, you would not find it quite so light a labor. If you are ever brought into deep mire, where there is no possibility of standing, it is not so easy to put your feet on a rock, when the rock does not seem to be there. I find faith the easiest thing in the world to have when there is nothing in which to believe; but when I have room to exercise my faith, then I do not find I have as much strength to accomplish it.

STRENGTH

As I talked one day with a countryman, he used this description: "In the middle of winter I some-times think how well I could mow; and in early spring I think, oh, how I would like to reap! I feel ready for it. But when mowing time comes, and when reaping time comes, I find I do not have any strength to spare." So when you have no troubles, couldn't you mow them down at once? When you have no work to do, couldn't you do it? But when work and trouble come, you find how difficult they are.

Many Christians are like the stag who talked to itself, and said, "Why should I run away from the dogs? Look what a fine pair of horns I've got, and look what heels I've got, too. I might do these hounds some mischief. Why not stand and show them what I can do with my antlers? I can keep off any quantity of dogs." No sooner did the dogs bark than the stag took off running.

So it is with us. "Let sin arise," we say, "and we will soon rip it up and destroy it. Let trouble come, and we will soon get over it." But when sin and trouble come, we then find what our weakness is. Then we have to cry for the help of the Spirit. Through Him, we can do all things (Phil. 4:13); without Him, we can do nothing at all. In all the actions of the Christian's life, whether it is the act of consecrating one's self to Christ, the act of daily prayer, the act of constant submission, preaching the Gospel, ministering to the needs of the poor, or comforting the despondent—in all these things, the Christian finds his weakness and his powerlessness, unless he is clothed with the Spirit of God.

Effective Service

Why, I have been to see the sick at times, and I have thought how I would like to comfort them, but I could not get a word out that was worth their hearing, or worth my saying. My soul has been in agony to be the means of comforting a poor, sick, despondent brother, but I could do nothing. I left his room half wishing I had never been to see a sick person in my life. I have learned the lesson of my own inadequacy.

Often this same lesson is learned in preaching. You prepare a sermon, study it, and make the greatest mess in delivering it that can possibly be made. Then you say, "I wish I had never preached at all." But all this is to show us that neither in comforting nor in preaching can one do anything right, unless the Spirit works in us *"to will and to do of his good pleasure"* (Phil. 2:13). Moreover, everything that we do without the Spirit is unacceptable to God. Whatever we do under His influence, however we may despise it, is not despised by God. He never despises His own work or looks upon what He works in us with any other view than that of satisfaction and delight. If the Spirit helps me to groan, then God must accept the groaner. If you could pray the best prayer in the world without the Spirit, God would have nothing to do with it. But if your prayer is broken, lame, and limping, if the Spirit made it, God will look upon it and say, as He did upon the works of creation, "It is very good," and He will accept it.

FINAL CONSIDERATIONS

Let me conclude by asking this question: do you have the Spirit of God in you? You have some religion, most of you, I daresay. Well, of what kind is it? Is it a homemade article? Did you make yourself what you are? Then, if so, you are a lost person up to this moment. If, my friend, you have gone no further than you have walked yourself, you are not on the road to heaven yet; your face is turned the wrong way. But if you have received something that neither flesh nor blood could reveal to you, if you have been led to do the very thing that you once hated, and to love that thing that you once despised, and to despise that on which your heart and your pride were once set, then, soul, if this is the Spirit's work, rejoice; for where He has begun the good work He will carry it on (Phil. 1:6).

And you may know whether it is the Spirit's work by this: have you been led to Christ, and away from self? Have you been led away from all feelings, from all doings, from all willings, from all prayings, as the ground of your trust and your hope, and have you been brought nakedly to rely upon the finished work of Christ? If so, this is more than human nature ever taught any man; this is a height to which human nature never climbed. The Spirit of God has done this, and He will never leave what He has once begun, but you will *"go from strength to strength"* (Ps. 84:7), and you will stand among the blood-washed throng, at last complete in Christ, and *"accepted in the beloved"* (Eph. 1:6). But if you do not have the Spirit of Christ, you are none of His.

May the Spirit lead you to a quiet place where you can weep, repent, and look to Christ. May you now have a divine life implanted, which neither time nor eternity will be able to destroy. God, hear this prayer, and bless us for Jesus' sake. Amen.

Chapter 3

The Chief Office of the Holy Spirit

He shall glorify me: for he shall receive of mine, and shall show it unto you. All things that the Father hath are mine: therefore said I, that he shall take of mine, and shall show it unto you.
—John 16:14–15

I t is the chief office of the Holy Spirit to glorify Christ. He does many things, but this is what He aims at in all of them: to glorify Christ. Brethren, what the Holy Spirit does must be right for us to imitate; therefore, let us endeavor to glorify Christ. To what higher end can we devote ourselves than to something to which God the Holy Spirit devotes Himself? Let this be, then, your fervent prayer, "Blessed Spirit, help me ever to glorify the Lord Jesus Christ!"

Observe that the Holy Spirit glorifies Christ by showing the things of Christ to us. It is a great marvel that there should be any glory given to Christ by showing Him to such poor creatures as we. What! To make us see Christ, does this glorify Him? For our weak eyes to behold Him, for our trembling hearts to know Him and to love Him, does this glorify Him? Yes, it is so, for the Holy Spirit chooses this as His principal way of glorifying the Lord Jesus. He takes of the things of Christ, not to show them to angels, not to write them in letters of fire across the brow of night, but to show them to us.

Within the little temple of a sanctified heart, Christ is praised, not so much by what we do or think, as by what we see. This puts great value on meditation, on the study of God's Word, and on silent thought under the teaching of the Holy Spirit, for Jesus says, *"He shall glorify me: for he shall receive of mine, and shall show it unto you."*

Here is a gospel word at the very outset of our sermon: poor sinner, conscious of your sin, it is possible for Christ to be glorified by His being shown to you. If you look to Him, if you see Him to be a suitable Savior, an all-sufficient Savior, if your mind's eye takes Him in, if He is effectually shown to you by the Holy Spirit, He is thereby glorified. Sinner, as you are, unworthy apparently to become the arena of Christ's glory, yet will you be a temple in which the King's glory will be revealed, and your poor heart, like a mirror, will reflect His grace.

> Come, Holy Spirit, heavenly Dove,
> With all Your quickening powers.

Show Christ to the sinner that Christ may be glorified in the sinner's salvation!

If that great work of grace is really done at the beginning of the sermon, I will not mind if I never finish this message. God the Holy Spirit will have accomplished more without me than I could possibly have done myself, and to the Triune Jehovah will be all the praise. Oh, that the name of Christ may be glorified in every one of you! Has the Holy Spirit shown you Christ, the Sin-Bearer, the one sacrifice for sin, exalted on high to give repentance and remission? If so, then the Holy Spirit has glorified Christ, even in you.

Now proceeding to examine the text a little in detail, my first observation is this: the Holy Spirit is our Lord's Glorifier: *"He shall glorify me."* Second, Christ's own things are His best glory: *"He shall glorify me: for he shall receive of mine, and shall show it unto you."* Third, Christ's glory is His Father's glory: *"All things that the Father hath are mine: therefore said I, that he shall take of mine, and shall show it unto you."*

THE HOLY SPIRIT IS OUR LORD'S GLORIFIER

I want you to keep this truth in your mind and never forget it; what does not glorify Christ is not of the Holy Spirit, and what is of the Holy Spirit invariably glorifies our Lord Jesus Christ.

IN ALL COMFORTS

First, then, have an eye to this truth in all comforts. If a comfort that you think you need, and that appears to you to be very sweet, does not glorify Christ, look very suspiciously at it. If, in conversing with an apparently religious man, he chatters about truth that he says is comforting, but that does not honor Christ, do not have anything to do with it. It is a poisonous sweet; it may charm you for a moment, but it will ruin your soul forever if you partake of it.

But blessed are those comforts that smell of Christ; those consolations in which there is a fragrance *"of myrrh, and aloes, and cassia"* (Ps. 45:8), out of the King's palace; the comfort drawn from His person, His work, His blood, His resurrection, and His glory; the comfort directly derived from that sacred spot where He trod *"the winepress alone"* (Isa. 63:3). This is wine of which you may drink and forget your misery and be unhappy no more.

But always look with great suspicion upon any comfort offered to you, either as a sinner or a saint, that does not come distinctly from Christ. Say, "I will not be comforted until Jesus comforts me. I will refuse to lay aside my despondency until He removes my sin. I will not go to Mr. Civility or Mr. Legality for the unloading of my burden. No hands will ever lift the load of conscious sin from my heart but those that were nailed to the cross, when Jesus Himself bore my *"sins in his own body on the tree"* (1 Pet. 2:24). Please carry this truth with you wherever you go, as a kind of spiritual litmus paper, by which you may test everything that is presented to you as a help or comfort. If it does not glorify Christ, let it not console or please you.

In All Ministries

In the next place, have an eye to this truth in all ministries. There are many ministries in the world, and they are very different from one another, but this truth will enable you to judge which are right out of them all. The ministries that make much of Christ are of the Holy Spirit, and the ministries that discredit Him, ignore Him, or put Him in the background in any degree are not of the Spirit of God.

Any doctrine that magnifies man, but not man's Redeemer, any doctrine that denies the depth of the Fall, and consequently detracts from the greatness of salvation, any doctrine that makes man sinless, and therefore makes Christ's work less—away with it, away with it! This will be an infallible test as to whether it is of the Holy Spirit or not, for Jesus says, *"He shall glorify me."*

It would be better to speak five words to the glory of Christ than to be the greatest orator who ever lived or to neglect or dishonor the Lord Jesus Christ. We who are preachers of the Word have but a short time to live; let us dedicate all that time to the glorious work of magnifying Christ.

Longfellow says in his poem "A Psalm of Life," "Art is long," but longer still is the great art of lifting up the Crucified before the eyes of the sin-bitten sons of men. Let us keep to that one employment. If we have but this one string upon which we can play, we may create such music on it that would ravish angels and would save men; therefore, again I say, let us keep to that alone. *"Cornet, flute, harp, sackbut, psaltery, dulcimer, and all kinds of music"* (Dan. 3:5) called the people to worship Nebuchadnezzar's golden image; but, as for worshipping our God, our one harp is Christ Jesus. We will touch every string of that wondrous instrument, even though it is with trembling fingers, and marvelous will be the music we will evoke from it.

All ministries, therefore, must be subjected to this test; if they do not glorify Christ, they are not of the Holy Spirit.

IN ALL RELIGIOUS MOVEMENTS

We should also have an eye to this truth in all religious movements and judge them by this standard. If they are of the Holy Spirit, they glorify Christ. There are great movements in the world every now and then. We are inclined to look upon them hopefully, for any stir is better than stagnation, but, before long, we begin to fear with a holy jealousy what their effects will be. How will we judge them? To what test will we put them? Always to this test: does this movement glorify Christ? Is Christ preached? Then therein I rejoice, yes, and will rejoice.

Are men pointed to Christ? Then this is the ministry of salvation. Is He preached as First and Last? Are men invited to be justified by faith in Him, and then to follow Him and copy His divine example? It is well.

I do not believe that any man ever lifted up the cross of Christ in a hurtful way. If only the cross is seen, it is the sight of the cross, not of the hands that lift it, that will bring salvation.

Some modern movements are heralded with great noise, and some come quietly, but if they glorify Christ, it is well. But, dear friends, if it is some new theory that is propounded, if it is some old error revived, if it is something very glittering and fascinating, and for a while it attracts the multitudes, think nothing of it; unless it glorifies Christ, it is not for you and me. *"Aliquid Christi,"* as one of the old fathers said, "Anything of Christ," and I love it. But if something has nothing of Christ, or something against Christ, then it may be very fine and flowery, and it may be very fascinating and charming, highly poetical, and in harmony with the spirit of the age, but we say of it, *"'Vanity of vanities; all is vanity'* (Eccl. 1:2) where there is no Christ."

Where He is uplifted, there is all that is needed for the salvation of a guilty race. Judge every movement, then, not by those who adhere to it, nor by those who admire and praise it, but by this word of our Lord, *"He shall glorify me."* The Spirit of God is not in it if it does not glorify Christ.

IN PHYSICAL, MENTAL, OR SPIRITUAL WEAKNESS

Once again, brethren, I pray that you would consider this truth when you are under a sense of great weakness, either physical, mental, or spiritual. You have finished preaching a sermon, you have completed a time of distributing tracts, or you have ended your Sunday school work for another Sabbath. You say to yourself, "I fear that I have done very poorly." You groan as you go to your bed because you think that you have not glorified Christ. It is good for you to groan if that is the case. I will not forbid it, but I will relieve the bitterness of your distress by reminding you that it is the Holy Spirit who is to glorify Christ: *"He shall glorify me."*

If I preach and the Holy Spirit is with me, Christ will be glorified; but if I were able to *"speak with the tongues of men and of angels"* (1 Cor. 13:1), yet without the power of the Holy Spirit, Christ would not be glorified. Sometimes, our weakness may even help to make way for the greater display of the might of God. If so, we may glory in infirmity, *"that the power of Christ may rest upon* [us]" (2 Cor. 12:9). It is not merely we who speak, but the Spirit of the Lord who speaks through us.

There is *"a sound of abundance of rain"* (1 Kings 18:41) outside the tabernacle; oh, that there were also the sound of abundance of rain within our hearts! May the Holy Spirit come at this moment, and come at all times whenever His servants are trying to glorify Christ. May He do what must always be His own work!

How can you and I glorify anybody, much less glorify Him who is infinitely glorious? But the Holy Spirit, being Himself the glorious God, can glorify the glorious Christ. It is a work worthy of God, and it shows us, when we think of it, the absolute need of our crying to the Holy Spirit that He would take us in His hand and use us as a workman uses his hammer. What can a hammer do without the hand that grasps it, and what can we do without the Spirit of God?

IN TRIALS

I will make only one more observation upon this first point. If the Holy Spirit is to glorify Christ, I beg you to have an eye to this truth amid all oppositions, controversies, and contentions: if we alone had the task of glorifying Christ, we might be beaten; but since the Holy Spirit is the Glorifier of Christ, His glory is in very safe hands.

"Why do the heathen rage, and the people imagine a vain thing?" (Ps. 2:1). The Holy Spirit is still on the front lines. The eternal purpose of God to set His King upon the throne and to make Jesus Christ reign forever and ever must be fulfilled, for the Holy Spirit has undertaken to see it accomplished. Amid the surging tumults of the battle, the result of the conflict is never in doubt for a moment. It may seem as though the fate of Christ's cause hung in the balance, and that the scales were in equilibrium, but it is not so. The glory of Christ never wanes; it must increase from day to day, as it is made known in the hearts of men by the Holy Spirit; and the day will

come when Christ's praise will go up from all human tongues. Every knee will bow to Him (Phil. 2:10), and *"every tongue* [will] *confess that Jesus Christ is Lord, to the glory of God the Father"* (v. 11). Therefore, *"lift up the hands which hang down, and the feeble knees"* (Heb. 12:12).

If you have failed to glorify Christ by your speech as you would, there is Another who has done it, and who will still do it, according to Christ's words, *"He shall glorify me."* My text seems to be a silver bell, ringing sweet comfort into the dispirited Christian worker's ear. *"He shall glorify me."* That is the first point, that the Holy Spirit is our Lord's Glorifier. Keep that truth before your mind's eye under all circumstances.

CHRIST'S OWN THINGS ARE HIS BEST GLORY

When the Holy Spirit wants to glorify Christ, what does He do? He does not go abroad for anything; He comes to Christ Himself for that which will be for Christ's own glory: *"He shall glorify me: for he shall receive of mine, and shall show it unto you."* There can be no glory added to Christ; it must be His own glory, which He has already, which is made more apparent to the hearts of God's chosen by the Holy Spirit.

NOTHING NEW IS NEEDED

First of all, Christ needs no new inventions to glorify Him. "We have invented a new line of things," says one. Have you? "We have discovered something very wonderful." I daresay you have, but Christ, *"the same yesterday, today, and forever"* (Heb. 13:8 NKJV), needs none of your inventions, discoveries, or additions to His truth. A plain Christ is forever the loveliest Christ. Dress Him up, and you have deformed Him and defamed Him. Bring Him out just as He is, the Christ of God, nothing else but Christ, unless you bring in His Cross, for *"we preach Christ crucified"* (1 Cor. 1:23); indeed, you cannot have Christ without the Cross; but preach Christ crucified, and you have given Him all the glory that He desires. The Holy Spirit does not reveal in these last times any fresh laws or any novel doctrines or any new evolutions. He simply brings to mind the things that Christ Himself spoke. He brings Christ's own things to us, and in that way glorifies Him.

HIS PERSON

Think for a minute of Christ's person as revealed to us by the Holy Spirit. What can more glorify Him than for us to see His person, very God of very God, and yet as truly man? What a wondrous being, as human as ourselves, but as divine as God! Was there ever another like Him? Never. Think of His incarnation, His birth at Bethlehem. There was greater glory among the oxen in the stall than ever was seen where those born in marble halls were swathed in purple and fine linen. Was there ever another baby like Christ? Never. I am not surprised that the wise men fell down to worship Him.

HIS LIFE

Look at His life, the standing wonder of all ages. Men who have not worshipped Him have admired

Him. His life is incomparable, unique; there is nothing like it in all the history of mankind. Imagination has never been able to invent anything approximating the perfect beauty of the life of Jesus Christ.

HIS DEATH

Think of His death. There have been many heroic deaths and martyrdoms, but there is not one that can be set side by side with Christ's death. He did not pay the debt of nature as others do, and yet He paid our nature's debt. He did not die because He had to; He died because He would. The only "must" that came upon Him was a necessity of all-conquering love. The Cross of Christ is the greatest wonder of fact or fiction; fiction invents many marvelous things, but nothing that can be compared for a moment with the Cross of Christ.

HIS RESURRECTION

Think of our Lord's resurrection. If this is one of the things that are taken and shown to you by the Holy Spirit, it will fill you with holy delight. I am sure that I could go into that sepulchre, where John and Peter went, and spend a lifetime in revering Him who broke down the barrier of the tomb and made it a passageway to heaven. Instead of its being a dungeon and a cul-de-sac, into which all men seem to go, but could never come out of, Christ has, by His resurrection, made a tunnel right through the grave. Jesus, by dying, has killed death for all believers.

HIS ASCENSION

Then think of His ascension. But why do I need to take you over all these scenes with which you are blessedly familiar? What a wondrous fact that, when the cloud received Him out of the disciples' sight, the angels came to accompany Him to His heavenly home!

> They brought His chariot from above,
> To bear Him to His throne;
> Clapp'd their triumphant wings, and cried,
> "The glorious work is done."

HIS SECOND COMING

Think of Him now, at His Father's right hand, adored of all the heavenly host; then let your mind fly forward to the glory of His Second Advent, the final judgment with its terrible terrors, the Millennium with its indescribable bliss, and the heaven of heavens with its endless and unparalleled splendor. If these things are shown to you by the Holy Spirit, the beatific vision will indeed glorify Christ, and you will sit down and sing with the blessed Virgin, *"My soul magnifies the Lord, and my spirit has rejoiced in God my Savior"* (Luke 1:46 NKJV).

Thus you see that the things that glorify Christ are all in Christ; the Holy Spirit brings nothing from abroad, but He takes of the things of Christ and shows them to us. The glory of kings lies in their silver and gold, their silk and gems, but the glory of Christ lies in Himself.

If we want to glorify a man, we bring Him presents; if we wish to glorify Christ, we must accept presents from Him. Thus we take the cup of salvation, calling upon the name of the Lord, and, in so doing, we glorify Christ.

THE SPIRIT MUST REVEAL CHRIST

Notice next that these things of Christ's are too bright for us to see until the Spirit shows them to us. We cannot see them because of their excessive glory, until the Holy Spirit tenderly reveals them to us, until He takes the things of Christ and shows them to us.

HE ENLIGHTENS THE ABILITY TO UNDERSTAND

What does this mean? Does it not mean, first, that He enlightens our understanding? It is wonderful how the Holy Spirit can take a fool and make him know the wonders of Christ's dying love; He makes him know it very quickly when He begins to teach him. Some of us have been very slow learners, yet the Holy Spirit has been able to teach something even to us. He opens the Scriptures, and He also opens our minds; and when there are these two openings together, what a wonderful opening it is! It becomes like a new revelation; the first is the revelation of the letter, which we have in the Book; the second is the revelation of the Spirit, which we get in our own spirits. Friend, if the Holy Spirit has ever enlightened your understanding, you know what it is for Him to show the things of Christ to you!

HE TOUCHES THE SOUL

He does this by a work upon the whole soul. I mean this: when the Holy Spirit convinces us of sin, we become equipped to see Christ, and so the blessed Spirit shows Christ to us. When we are conscious of our feebleness, then we see Christ's strength; thus, the Holy Spirit shows Him to us. Often the operations of the Spirit of God may not seem to include directly showing Christ to us, but as they prepare us for seeing Him, they are a part of the work.

HE BRINGS TRUTH TO LIFE

The Holy Spirit sometimes shows Christ to us by His power of vivifying the truth. I have sometimes seen a truth differently from what I have ever seen it before. I knew it long ago. I owned it as part of the divine revelation. But now I realize it, grip it, grasp it; or what is better, it seems to get a grip on me and hold me in its mighty hands. Have you not sometimes been overjoyed with a promise that never seemed anything to you before? Or has a doctrine that you believed, but never fully appreciated, suddenly become to you a gem of the purest luster, a very Koh-i-noor,[*] which means "mountain of light"? The Holy Spirit has a way of focusing light, and when it falls in this special way upon a certain point, then the truth is revealed to us. He will take the things of Christ and show them to you. Have you never felt ready to jump for joy, ready to rise from your seat, ready to sit up in your bed at night and sing praises to God through the overpowering influence of some grand old truth that has seemed to be all at once quite new to you?

HE USES LIFE EXPERIENCE

The Holy Spirit also shows to us the things of Christ in our experiences. As we journey on in life,

---

[*] A diamond acquired by the British, which became the central stone in the queen's crown and was worn by Queen Elizabeth at her coronation in 1937.

we pass up hill and down dale, through bright sunlight and through dark shadows, and in each of these conditions, we learn a little more of Christ, a little more of His grace, a little more of His glory, a little more of His sin-bearing, a little more of His glorious righteousness. Blessed is the life that is one long lesson on the glory of Christ. I think that is what every Christian's life should be. "Every dark and bending line" in our experience should meet in the center of Christ's glory and should lead us nearer and nearer to the power of enjoying the bliss at His right hand forever and ever. Thus the Holy Spirit takes of the things of Christ and shows them to us, and so glorifies Christ.

RESPOND TO THE HOLY SPIRIT'S LEADINGS

Beloved, the practical lesson for us to learn is this: let us try to abide under the influence of the Holy Spirit. To that end, let us think very reverently of Him. Some never think of Him at all. How many sermons there are without even an allusion to Him! Shame on the preachers of such discourses! If any hearers come without praying for the Holy Spirit, shame on such hearers! We know and we confess that He is everything to our spiritual lives; then why do we not remember Him with greater love, worship Him with greater honor, and think of Him continually with greater reverence?

Beware of committing the sin against the Holy Spirit. If you feel any gentle touches of His power when you are hearing a sermon, beware lest you harden your heart against them. Whenever the sacred fire comes as but a spark, *"quench not the Spirit"* (1 Thess. 5:19), but pray that the spark may become a flame.

And you, Christian people, cry to Him that you may not read your Bibles without His light. Do not pray without being helped by the Spirit. Above all, may you never preach without the Holy Spirit! It seems a pity when a man asks to be guided of the Spirit in his preaching, and then pulls out a manuscript and reads it. The Holy Sprit may bless what the minister reads, but He cannot very well guide him when he has tied himself down to what he has written. And it will be the same with the speaker if he only repeats what he has learned and leaves no room for the Spirit to give him a new thought or a fresh revelation of Christ. How can he hope for the divine blessing under such circumstances? Oh, it would be better for us to sit still until some of us were moved by the Spirit to get up and speak than for us to prescribe the methods by which He should speak to us, and even to write down the very words we mean to utter! What room is there for the Spirit's operations then?

"Come, Holy Spirit, heavenly Dove." I cannot help breaking out into that prayer. "Blessed Spirit, abide with us, take of the things of Christ and show them to us so that Christ may be glorified."

CHRIST'S GLORY IS HIS FATHER'S GLORY

The last point is a very deep one, much too deep for me. I am unable to take you into the depths of my text. I will not pretend to do so. I believe that there are meanings here that we will probably never understand until we get to heaven. *"Thou knowest not now; but thou shalt know hereafter"* (John 13:7). But this is the point: *"All things that the Father hath are mine: therefore said I, that he shall take of mine, and shall show it unto you."*

CHRIST HAS ALL THE FATHER HAS

First, Christ has all that the Father has. Think about that. No more can any man dare to say, *"All things that the Father hath are mine."* All the Godhead is in Christ; not only all the attributes of it, but also the essence of it. The Nicene Creed puts it well, and it is not too strong to say it this way, "Light of Light, very God of very God," for Christ has all that the Father has. When we come to Christ, we come to omnipotent, omnipresent omniscience; we come to almighty immutability; we come, in fact, to the eternal Godhead. The Father has all things, and all power is given to Christ in heaven and on earth, so that He has all that the Father has.

GOD IS GLORIFIED IN CHRIST'S GLORY

Further, the Father is glorified in Christ's glory. Never let us fall into the false notion that if we magnify Christ, we are depreciating the Father. If any lips have ever spoken concerning the Christ of God so as to depreciate the God of Christ, let those lips be covered with shame. We never preached Christ as merciful, and the Father as only just, or Christ as moving the Father to be gracious. That is a slander that has been cast upon us, but there is not an atom of truth in it. We have known and believed what Christ Himself said, *"I and my Father are one"* (John 10:30).

The more glorious Christ is, the more glorious the Father is; and when men, professedly Christians, begin to cast off Christ, they cast off God the Father, to a large extent. Irreverence to the Son of God soon becomes irreverence to God the Father Himself. But, dear friends, we delight to honor Christ, and we will continue to do so. Even when we stand in the heaven of heavens, before the burning throne of the infinite Jehovah, we will sing praises to Him and to the Lamb, putting the Two evermore in that divine conjunction in which They are always to be found.

Thus, you see, Christ has all that the Father has, and when He is glorified, the Father is also glorified.

THE HOLY SPIRIT MUST REVEAL THE TRUTH TO US

Next, the Holy Spirit must lead us to see this, and I am sure that He will. If we give ourselves up to His teaching, we will fall into no errors. It will be a great mystery, but we will know enough so that it will never trouble us. If you sit down and try to study the mystery of the Eternal, well, I believe that the longer you look, the more you will be like persons who look into the sea from a great height, until they grow dizzy and are ready to fall and to be drowned.

Believe what the Spirit teaches you, and adore your divine Teacher; then His instruction will become easy to you. I believe that, as we grow older, we come to worship God as Abraham did, as Jehovah, the great I AM. Jesus does not fade into the background, but the glorious Godhead seems to become more and more apparent to us. As our Lord's words to His disciples state, *"Ye believe in God, believe also in me"* (John 14:1). And as we come to full confidence in the glorious Lord, the God of nature, of providence, of redemption, and of heaven, the Holy Spirit helps us to know more of the glories of Christ.

I have talked with you as well as I could upon this sublime theme, and if I did not know that the Holy Spirit glorifies Christ, I would go home miserable, for I have not been able to glorify my Lord as I wish I could. But I know that the Holy Spirit can take what I have said out of my very heart, can put it into your hearts, and can add to it whatever I have omitted. Go, you who love the Lord, and glorify Him. Try to do it by your lips and by your lives. Go and preach Him, preach more of Him, and lift Him up higher, higher, and higher.

I heard of an old lady who made a mistake in what she said, yet there was a truth behind her blunder. She had been to a little Baptist chapel, where a high Calvinist preached. On coming away she said that she liked "high Calvary" preachers best. So do I. Give me a "high Calvary" preacher, one who will make Calvary the highest of all the mountains. I suppose it was not a hill at all, but only a mound; still, let us lift it higher and higher, and say to all other hills, *"Why leap ye, ye high hills? this is the hill which God desireth to dwell in; yea, the LORD will dwell in it for ever"* (Ps. 68:16).

The crucified Christ is wiser than all the wisdom of the world. The Cross of Christ has more newness in it than all the fresh things of the earth. Oh, believers and preachers of the Gospel, glorify Christ! May the Holy Spirit help you to do so! And you, poor sinners, who think that you cannot glorify Christ at all, come and trust Him. "Come naked, come filthy, come just as you are," and believe that He will receive you, for that will glorify Him. Believe, even now, O sinner at death's door, that Christ can make you live, for your faith will glorify Him! Look up out of the awful depths of hell into which conscience has cast you, and believe that He can pluck you out of the *"horrible pit, out of the miry clay, and set* [your] *feet upon a rock"* (Ps. 40:2), for your trust will glorify Him! It is in the power of the sinner to give Christ the greatest glory, if the Holy Spirit enables him to believe in the Lord Jesus Christ. You may come, you who are more leprous, more diseased, more corrupt, than any other; if you look to Him, and He saves you, oh, then you will praise Him! You will be of the mind of the one I have spoken of many times, who said to me, "Sir, you say that Christ can save me. Well, if He does, He will never hear the last of it." No, and He never *will* hear the last of it. Blessed Jesus,

> I will love Thee in life, I will love Thee in death,
> And praise Thee as long as Thou lendest me breath;
> And say when the death-dew lies cold on my brow,
> If ever I loved Thee, my Jesus, 'tis now.
>
> In mansion of glory and endless delight,
> I'll ever adore Thee in heaven so bright;
> I'll sing with the glittering crown on my brow,
> If ever I loved thee, my Jesus, 'tis now.

We will do nothing else but praise Christ and glorify Him, if He will but save us from sin. God grant that it may be so with every one of us, for the Lord Jesus Christ's sake!

Chapter 4

The Personality of the Holy Spirit

And I will pray the Father, and he shall give you another Comforter, that he may abide with you for ever; even the Spirit of truth; whom the world cannot receive, because it seeth him not, neither knoweth him: but ye know him; for he dwelleth with you, and shall be in you.
—John 14:16–17

After reading the text, you will be surprised to know that I do not intend to say anything about the Holy Spirit as the Comforter. In this message, I will endeavor to explain and enforce certain other doctrines, which I believe are plainly taught in this text, and which I hope God the Holy Spirit may make profitable to our souls. Old John Newton once said that there were some books that he could not read. They were good and sound enough, but he said,

> They are books of halfpence; you have to take so much in quantity before you have any value; there are other books of silver, and others of gold; but I have one book that is a book of banknotes; and every leaf is a banknote of immense value.

72

I have found this to be true with this text. I have a banknote of so large a sum that I could not tell its whole worth in this one message. I would have to write many chapters before I could unfold to you the whole value of this precious promise—one of the last that Christ gave to His people.

I invite your attention to this passage because we will find in it some instruction on four points: first, concerning the true and proper personality of the Holy Spirit; second, concerning the united agency of the glorious Three persons in the work of our salvation; third, something to establish the doctrine of the indwelling of the Holy Spirit in the souls of all believers; fourth, we will find out the reason the carnal mind rejects the Holy Spirit.

THE PERSON OF THE HOLY SPIRIT

We are so accustomed to talk about the influence of the Holy Spirit and His sacred operations and graces that we are apt to forget that the Holy Spirit is truly and actually a person—that He is a subsistence—an existence, or, as we Trinitarians usually say, one person in the essence of the Godhead.

I am afraid that, though we do not know it, we have acquired the habit of regarding the Holy Spirit as an emanation flowing from the Father and the Son, but not as being actually a person Himself. I know it is not easy to carry about in our minds the idea of the Holy Spirit as a person.

I can think of the Father as a person, because His acts are such as I can understand. I see Him hang the world in ether. I behold Him swaddling a newborn sea in bands of darkness. I know it is He who formed the drops of hail, who led forth the stars by their hosts, and called them by their names. I can conceive of Him as a person, because I can observe His operations.

I can realize that Jesus, the Son of Man, is a real person, because He is bone of my bone and flesh of my flesh. It takes no great stretch of my imagination to picture the babe in Bethlehem, or to behold the *"man of sorrows,...acquainted with grief"* (Isa. 53:3), or the King of martyrs, as He was persecuted in Pilate's hall or nailed to the accursed tree for our sins. Nor do I find it difficult at times to realize the person of my Jesus sitting on His throne in heaven or encircled with clouds and wearing the diadem of all creation, calling the earth to judgment and summoning us to hear our final sentences.

But when I come to deal with the Holy Spirit, His operations are so mysterious, His doings are so secret, His acts are so removed from everything that is of sense, and of the body, that I cannot so easily grasp the idea of His being a person—but a person He is. God the Holy Spirit is not an influence, an emanation, a stream of something flowing from the Father, but He is as much an actual person as either God the Son or God the Father. I will attempt to establish the doctrine, and to show you the truth of it, that God the Holy Spirit is actually a person.

BAPTISM

The first proof we will gather from the pool of holy baptism. Let me take you down, as I have taken others, into the pool, now concealed, but which I wish were always open to your view. Let me take you to the baptismal font, where believers put on the name of the Lord Jesus, and you will hear me pronounce the solemn words, "I baptize thee in the name"—mark, "in the name," not names—"of the Father, and of the Son, and of the Holy Spirit." Everyone who is baptized according to the true form laid down in Scripture must be a Trinitarian; otherwise, his baptism is a farce and a lie, and he himself is found to be a deceiver and a hypocrite before God.

As the Father is mentioned, and as the Son is mentioned, so is the Holy Spirit; and the whole is summed up as being a Trinity in unity, by its being said, not the names, but "the name," the glorious name, the Jehovah name, "of the Father, and of the Son, and of the Holy Spirit."

BENEDICTION

Let me remind you that the same thing often occurs when you are dismissed from the house of prayer. In pronouncing the solemn closing benediction, the minister invokes on your behalf the love of Jesus Christ, the grace of the Father, and the fellowship of the Holy Spirit. Thus, according to the apostolic manner, he makes a manifest distinction among the persons, showing that we believe the Father to be a person, the Son to be a person, and the Holy Spirit to be a person. Were there no other proofs in Scripture, I think these would be sufficient for every sensible man. He would see that if the Holy Spirit were a mere influence, He would not be mentioned in conjunction with Two whom we all confess to be actual and proper persons.

APPEARANCES

Another argument arises from the fact that the Holy Spirit has actually made different appearances on earth. The Great Spirit has manifested Himself to man. He has put on a form, so that, while He has not been seen by mortal men, He has been so veiled in appearance that He was seen, so far as that appearance was concerned, by the eyes of all beholders. Do you see Jesus Christ our Savior? There is the river Jordan, with its shelving banks and its willows weeping at its side. Jesus Christ, the Son of God, descends into the stream, and the holy Baptist, John, plunges Him into the waves. The doors of heaven are opened. A miraculous appearance presents itself. A bright light shines from the sky, brighter than the sun in all its grandeur, and down in a flood of glory descends something that you recognize to be a dove. It rests on Jesus. It sits upon His sacred head, and as the old painters put a halo around the brow of Jesus, so did the Holy Spirit shed a resplendence around the face of Him who came to fulfill all righteousness, and therefore commenced with the ordinance of baptism. The Holy Spirit was seen as a dove, to mark His purity and His gentleness, and He came down like a dove from heaven to show that it is from heaven alone that He descends.

Nor was this the only time when the Holy Spirit has been manifest in a visible shape. Can you envision that company of disciples gathered together in an upper room? They are waiting for some promised blessing, and, before long, it will come. Listen! There is a sound *"as of a rushing mighty wind"* (Acts 2:2). It fills all the house where they are sitting (v. 2); and astonished, they look around them, wondering what will come next. Soon a bright light appears, shining upon the heads of each. Cloven tongues of fire rest upon them (v. 3). What were these marvelous appearances of wind and flame but a display of the Holy Spirit in His proper person? The fact of an appearance manifests that He must be a person. An "influence" could not appear; an "attribute" could not appear. We cannot see attributes, and we cannot behold influences. The Holy Spirit must, then, be a person, since He was beheld by mortal eyes, and He came under the cognizance of mortal sense.

Human Characteristics

Another proof is that personal qualities are, in Scripture, ascribed to the Holy Spirit.

Understanding

First, let us consider a text in which the Holy Spirit is spoken of as having understanding.

> But as it is written, Eye hath not seen, nor ear heard, neither have entered into the heart of man, the things which God hath prepared for them that love him. But God hath revealed them unto us by his Spirit: for the Spirit searcheth all things, yea, the deep things of God. For what man knoweth the things of a man, save the spirit of man which is in him? even so the things of God knoweth no man, but the Spirit of God.   (1 Cor. 2:9–11)

Here you see an understanding—a power of knowledge is ascribed to the Holy Spirit. Now, if

there are any persons whose minds are of so prepos-
terous a complexion that they would ascribe one attribute to another, and would speak of a mere
influence as having understanding, then I give up all
the argument. But I believe every rational man will
admit that, when anything is spoken of as having an
understanding, it must be an existence. It must, in
fact, be a person.

WILL

In the same epistle, you find a will ascribed to
the Holy Spirit. *"But all these worketh that one and
the selfsame Spirit, dividing to every man severally
as he will"* (1 Cor. 12:11). So it is plain that the
Spirit has a will. He does not come from God simply
at God's will, but He has a will of His own, which is
always in keeping with the will of the infinite Jehovah; nevertheless, it is distinct and separate. Therefore, I say He is a person.

POWER

In another text, power is ascribed to the Holy
Spirit, and power is a thing that can only be ascribed
to an existence. Romans 15:13 reads, *"Now the God
of hope fill you with all joy and peace in believing,
that ye may abound in hope, through the power of the
Holy Ghost."* I need not insist upon it, because it is
self-evident, that wherever you find understanding,
will, and power, you must also find an existence. It
cannot be a mere attribute. It cannot be a metaphor.
It cannot be a personified influence. It must be a
person. But I have a proof that, perhaps, will be
more telling upon you than any other.

Actions and Deeds

Actions and deeds are ascribed to the Holy Spirit; therefore, He must be a person. You read in the first chapter of the book of Genesis that the Spirit hovered over the surface of the earth, when it was as yet all disorder and confusion (v. 2 NKJV). This world was once a mass of chaotic matter with no order. It was like the valley of darkness and of the shadow of death. God the Holy Spirit spread His wings over it. He sowed the seeds of life in it. The germs from which all beings sprang were implanted by Him. He impregnated the earth so that it became capable of life.

Now, it must have been a person who brought order out of confusion. It must have been an existence who hovered over this world and made it what it is now. But do we not read in Scripture something more of the Holy Spirit? Yes, we are told that *"holy men of God spoke as they were moved by the Holy Spirit"* (2 Pet. 1:21 NKJV). When Moses penned the Pentateuch, the Holy Spirit moved his hand. When David wrote the Psalms and created sweet music on his harp, it was the Holy Spirit who gave his fingers their seraphic motion. When Solomon dropped from his lips the words of the proverbs of wisdom, or when he hymned the canticles of love, it was the Holy Spirit who gave him the words of knowledge and hymns of rapture. Ah, what fire was it that touched the lips of the eloquent Isaiah? What hand was it that came upon Daniel? What might was it that made Jeremiah so plaintive in his grief? What was it that lifted Ezekiel and made him fly like an eagle, soaring into mysteries aloft and seeing the mighty unknown beyond our reach? Who was it that made Amos, the herdsman, a prophet? Who taught the rugged Haggai to pronounce his thundering sentences? Who showed Habakkuk the horses of Jehovah marching through the waters? Who kindled the burning eloquence of Nahum? Who caused Malachi to close his book with the mention of the word *"curse"?* Who was it in each of these, except the Holy Spirit?

Must it not have been a person who spoke in and through these ancient witnesses? We must believe it. We cannot avoid believing it, when we read that *"holy men of God spoke as they were moved by the Holy Spirit"* (2 Pet. 1:21 NKJV).

And when has the Holy Spirit ceased to have an influence upon men? We find that He still deals with His ministers and with all His saints. Turn to the book of Acts, and you will find that the Holy Spirit said, *"Separate me Barnabas and Saul for the work"* (Acts 13:2). I never heard of an *attribute* saying such a thing. The Holy Spirit said to Peter, "Go to the centurion, and do not call common or unclean what I have cleansed." (See Acts 10.) The Holy Spirit *"caught away Philip"* after he had baptized the eunuch and carried him away to another place (Acts 8:38–40), and the Holy Spirit said to Paul *"that he should not go up to Jerusalem"* (Acts 21:4). And we know that the Holy Spirit was lied to by Ananias and Sapphira, when Peter said, *"Thou hast not lied unto men, but unto God"* (Acts 5:4). Again, that power that we feel every day, those of us who are called to preach; that wondrous spell that makes our lips so potent; that power that gives us thoughts that are like birds from a far-off region, not the natives of our soul; that influence that I sometimes strangely feel, which, if it does not give me poetry and eloquence, gives me a might I never felt before and lifts me above my fellowman; that majesty with which He clothes His ministers, until in the midst of the battle they cry along with Job *"things too wonderful"* (Job 42:3) and move themselves like leviathans in the water; that power that gives us might over men, and causes them to sit and listen as if their ears were chained, as if they were entranced by the power of some magician's wand—that power must come from a person; it must come from the Holy Spirit.

But is it not said in Scripture, and do we not feel it, dear friends, that it is the Holy Spirit who regenerates the soul? It is the Holy Spirit who quickens us. *"You hath he quickened, who were dead in trespasses and sins"* (Eph. 2:1). It is the Holy Spirit who imparts the first germ of life, convincing us of sin, of righteousness, and of judgment to come (John 16:8). And is it not the Holy Spirit who, after that flame is kindled, still fans it with the breath of His mouth and keeps it alive? Its Author is its Preserver. Oh, can it be said that it is the Holy Spirit who strives in men's souls? That it is the Holy Spirit who brings them into the sweet place that is called Calvary? Can it be said that He does all these things, and yet is not a person? It may be said, but it must be said by fools; for one can never be a wise man who can consider that these things can be done by any other than a glorious person—a divine existence.

EMOTIONS

Allow me to give you one more proof. Certain feelings are ascribed to the Holy Spirit that can be understood only upon the supposition that He actually is a person. Ephesians 4:30 states that the Holy Spirit can be grieved: *"Grieve not the holy Spirit of God, whereby ye are sealed unto the day of redemption."* In Isaiah 63:10, we read that the Holy Spirit can be vexed: *"But they rebelled, and vexed his holy Spirit: therefore he was turned to be their enemy, and he fought against them."* Acts 7:51 tells us that the Holy Spirit can be resisted: *"Ye stiffnecked and uncircumcised in heart and ears, ye do always resist the Holy Ghost: as your fathers did, so do ye."* And in Acts 5:9, we find that the Holy Spirit may be tempted. We are informed that Peter said to Ananias and Sapphira, *"How is it that ye have agreed together to tempt the Spirit of the Lord?"*

Now, these things could not be emotions that might be ascribed to a quality or an emanation. They must be understood to relate to a person. An influence could not be grieved; it must be a person who can be grieved, vexed, or resisted. And now, dear ones, I think I have fully established the point of the personality of the Holy Spirit.

Please permit me now, most earnestly, to impress upon you the absolute necessity of being sound on the doctrine of the Trinity. I knew a man, a good minister of Jesus Christ he is now, and I believe he was before he turned his eyes unto heresy. He began to doubt the glorious divinity of our blessed Lord, and for years he preached the unorthodox doctrine, until one day he happened to hear a very eccentric old minister preaching from the text,

But there the glorious LORD will be unto us a place of broad rivers and streams; wherein

> *shall go no galley with oars, neither shall gal-*
> *lant ship pass thereby....Thy tacklings are*
> *loosed; they could not well strengthen their*
> *mast, they could not spread the sail.*
>
> (Isa. 33:21, 23)

"Now," said the old minister, "you give up the Trinity, and your tacklings are loosed; you cannot strengthen your masts. Once you give up the doctrine of the Three persons, and your tacklings are all gone, your mast, which ought to be a support to your vessel, is a rickety one, and it shakes."

A Gospel without the Trinity! It is a pyramid built upon its apex. A Gospel without the Trinity! It is a rope of sand that cannot hold together. A Gospel without the Trinity! Then, indeed, Satan can overturn it. But give me a Gospel with the Trinity, and the might of hell cannot prevail against it. No man can anymore overthrow it than a bubble could split a rock, or a feather break a mountain in two.

Grasp the thought of the Three persons, and you have the marrow of all divinity. Only know the Father, and know the Son, and know the Holy Spirit to be one, and all things will appear clear. This is the golden key to the secrets of nature. This is the silken clue of the labyrinths of mystery, and he who understands this will soon understand as much as mortals can ever know.

THE UNITED AGENCY OF THE TRINITY

Now we come to our second point: the united agency of the Three persons in the work of our salvation. Look at the text, and you will find all three persons of the Trinity mentioned. *"I"*—that is the Son—

"will pray the Father, and he shall give you another Comforter." There the Three persons are mentioned, all of them doing something for our salvation. *"I will pray,"* says the Son. "I will send," says the Father. "I will comfort," says the Holy Spirit.

Now, let us, for a few moments, focus on this wondrous theme: the unity of the Three persons with regard to the great purpose of the salvation of the elect. When God first made man, He said, *"Let **us*** [not "let Me"] *make man"* (Gen. 1:26, emphasis added). The covenant Elohim said to each other, "Let Us unitedly become the creator of man."

So, when in the eternal ages of long ago, they said, "Let Us save man," it was not the Father who said, "Let Me save man," but the Three persons conjointly who said, with one consent, "Let Us save man." It is a source of sweet comfort to me to think that it is not only one person of the Trinity who is engaged for my salvation, it is not simply one person of the Godhead who vows that He will redeem me, but it is a glorious trio of divine ones, and the Three declare, unitedly, "We will save man."

Now, observe here that each person is spoken of as performing a separate office. *"I will pray,"* says the Son; that is intercession. "I will send," says the Father; that is donation. "I will comfort," says the Holy Spirit; that is supernatural influence. Oh, if it were possible for us to see the Three persons of the Godhead, we would behold one of them standing before the throne, with outstretched hands, crying day and night, "O Lord, how long?" We would see him girded with Urim and Thummim, precious stones on which were written the twelve names of the tribes of Israel. We would behold Him, crying unto His Father,

"Do not forget Your promises or Your covenant." We would hear Him make mention of our sorrows and speak of our griefs on our behalf, for He is our intercessor. And if we could see the Father, we would not see Him as a listless, idle spectator of the intercession of the Son, but we would see Him with attentive ear, listening to every word of Jesus and granting every petition.

Where is the Holy Spirit all the while? Is He idle? Oh, no! He is floating over the earth, and when He sees a weary soul, He says, "Come to Jesus; He will give you rest." When He beholds an eye filled with tears, He wipes away the tears and bids the mourner look for comfort at the Cross. When He sees the tempest-tossed believer, He takes the helm of his soul and speaks words of consolation. He helps the broken in heart and binds up their wounds, and, ever on His mission of mercy, He flies around the world, being present everywhere. Behold, how the Three persons work together.

Do not say, then, "I am grateful to the Son." Yes, you ought to be, but God the Son no more saves you than God the Father. Do not imagine that God the Father is a great tyrant, and that God the Son had to die to make Him merciful. It was not to make the Father love His people. Oh, no! One loves as much as the other; the Three are conjoined in the great purpose of rescuing the elect from damnation.

But notice another thing in the text that shows the blessed unity of the Three: the one person promises for the other. The Son says, *"I will pray the Father."* "Very well," the disciples may have said, "we can trust You for that." "And He will send you," Jesus continues. You see, here is the Son signing a bond on behalf of the Father. *"He shall give you another Comforter."* There is a bond on behalf of the Holy Spirit, too. "And He will abide with you forever."

One person speaks for the other; how could they, if there were any disagreement between them? If one wished to save, and the other did not, they could not promise on another's behalf. But whatever the Son says, the Father listens to; whatever the Father promises, the Holy Spirit works; and whatever the Holy Spirit injects into the soul, God the Father fulfills. So the Three together mutually promise on one another's behalf. There is a bond with three names attached—Father, Son, and Holy Spirit. By three immutable things, the Christian is secured beyond the reaches of death and hell. The Christian has a trinity of securities, because there is a Trinity in God.

THE INDWELLING OF THE HOLY SPIRIT

Our third point is the indwelling of the Holy Spirit in believers. Now, beloved, my first two points have been matters of pure doctrine; this point, however, is the subject of experience. The indwelling of the Holy Spirit is a subject so profound, and so having to do with the inner man, that no soul will be able truly and really to comprehend what I say, unless it has been taught of God.

I heard of an old minister who told a fellow of one of the Cambridge colleges that he understood a language that he never learned in all his life. "I have not," he said, "even a smattering of Greek, and I know no Latin. But thank God, I can talk the language of Canaan, and that is more than you can." So, beloved, I will now have to talk a little of the language of Canaan. If you cannot comprehend me, I am afraid it is because you are not of Israelite extraction; you are neither a child of God nor an inheritor of the kingdom of heaven.

We are told, in the text, that Jesus would send the Comforter, who would abide with the saints forever. He would dwell with them and be in them. Old Ignatius, the martyr, used to call himself Theophorus, or Godbearer, because, he said, "I bear about with me the Holy Spirit." And truly every Christian is a Godbearer. *"Know ye not that ye are the temple of God, and that the Spirit of God dwelleth in you?"* (1 Cor. 3:16).

A man is no Christian who does not have the Holy Spirit dwelling within him. He may speak well and understand theology. He may be a sound Calvinist. He may be a child of nature finely dressed, but not a child of the living God. He may be a man of so profound an intellect, so gigantic a soul, so comprehensive a mind, and so lofty an imagination that he may dive into all the secrets of nature. He may know the path that the eagle's eye has not seen and go into depths where the understanding of mortals does not reach, but he will not be a Christian, even with all of his knowledge. He will not be a son of God, with all his studies, unless he understands what it is to have the Holy Spirit dwelling and abiding in him forever.

Some people call this viewpoint fanaticism, and they say, "You are a Quaker; why not follow George Fox?" Well, we would not mind that much. We would follow anyone who followed the Holy Spirit. Even

Fox, with all his eccentricities, I do not doubt, was, in many cases, actually inspired by the Holy Spirit; and, whenever I find a man in whom there rests the Spirit of God, the Spirit within me leaps to hear the Spirit within him, and we feel that we are one. The Spirit of God in one Christian soul recognizes the Spirit in another.

I remember talking with a good man, as I believe he was, who insisted that it was impossible for us to know whether we had the Holy Spirit within us or not. I would like to read this verse to him, *"But ye know him; for he dwelleth with you, and shall be in you."*

Ah, do you think you cannot tell whether you have the Holy Spirit or not? Can I tell whether I am alive or not? If I were shocked by electricity, could I tell whether I was or not? I am sure I could! The shock would be strong enough to make me know where I stood. So, if I have God within me—if I have Deity tabernacling in my breast—if I have God the Holy Spirit resting in my heart and making a temple of my body, do you think I will know it? Call it fanaticism if you will, but I trust that there are some of us who know what it is to be always, or generally, under the influence of the Holy Spirit—always in one sense, generally in another. When we have difficulties, we ask the direction of the Holy Spirit. When we do not understand a portion of Holy Scripture, we ask God the Holy Spirit to shine upon us. When we are depressed, the Holy Spirit comforts us.

You cannot explain the wondrous power of the indwelling of the Holy Spirit—how it pulls back the hand of the saint when he would touch a forbidden thing; how it prompts him to make a covenant with his eyes; how it binds his feet, lest they should fall in a slippery way; how it restrains his heart and keeps him from temptation. Oh, you who know nothing of the indwelling of the Holy Spirit, do not despise it. Despise not the Holy Spirit, for that is the unpardonable sin.

> *Anyone who speaks a word against the Son of Man, it will be forgiven him; but whoever speaks against the Holy Spirit, it will not be forgiven him, either in this age or in the age to come.* (Matt. 12:32 NKJV)

Thus says the Word of God. Therefore tremble, lest in anything you despise the influences of the Holy Spirit.

Before closing this point, there is one little word that pleases me very much, and that is *forever*. You knew I would not miss that; you were certain I could not let it go without a comment. *"Abide with you for ever."* I wish I could get an Arminian* here to finish my sermon. I fancy I see him taking that word *forever*. He would stumble and say, "for...forever;" he would have to stammer and stutter, for he could never get it out all at once. At last, though, he would have to say, "The translation is wrong." And I suppose the poor man would have to prove that the original was wrong, too.

Ah, but blessed be God, we can read it! *"That he may abide with you for ever."* Give me the Holy

---

* Dutch theologian Jacob Arminius [1560–1609] opposed the Calvinists' beliefs in absolute predestination, irresistible grace, and the inability to fall from grace. Arminians believe in a conditional predestination and in man's ability to resist or respond to grace out of his free will.

Spirit, and I will never lose Him until *"for ever"* has run out, until eternity has spun its everlasting rounds.

WHY THE HOLY SPIRIT IS REJECTED BY SOME

Our text reads, *"Whom the world cannot receive, because it seeth him not, neither knoweth him."* You know what is sometimes meant by *"the world"*—those whom God in His wondrous sovereignty passed over when He chose His people—not the reprobates who were condemned to damnation by some awful decree, but those passed over by God, when He chose His elect. These cannot receive the Spirit. Again, it means all in a carnal state are not able to procure this divine influence for themselves; thus, it is true, *"Whom the world cannot receive."*

THE WORLD DOES NOT SEE HIM

The unregenerate world of sinners despises the Holy Spirit, *"because it seeth him not."* Yes, I believe this is the great secret why many laugh at the idea of the existence of the Holy Spirit—because they do not see Him. You tell the worldling, "I have the Holy Spirit within me." He says, "I cannot see it." He wants it to be something tangible, something he can recognize with his senses.

Have you ever heard the argument used by a good old Christian against an infidel doctor? The doctor said there is no soul, and asked, "Did you ever see a soul?"

"No," said the Christian.

"Did you ever hear a soul?"

"No."

"Did you ever smell a soul?"

"No."

"Did you ever taste a soul?"

"No."

"Did you ever feel a soul?"

"Yes," said the man. "I feel I have one within me."

"Well," said the doctor, "there are four senses against one; you have only one on your side."

"Very well," said the Christian, "Did you ever see a pain?"

"No."

"Did you ever hear a pain?"

"No."

"Did you ever smell a pain?"

"No."

"Did you ever taste a pain?"

"No."

"Did you ever feel a pain?"

"Yes."

"And that is quite enough, I suppose, to prove there is a pain?"

"Yes."

So the worldling says there is no Holy Spirit, because he cannot see it. Fine, but we feel it. You say that is fanaticism, and that we have never felt it. Suppose you tell me that honey is bitter. I reply, "No, I am sure you cannot have tasted it; taste it and try." So it is with the Holy Spirit. If you but once felt His influence, you would no longer say there is no Holy Spirit because you cannot see it.

Are there not many things, even in nature, that we cannot see? Did you ever see the wind? No, but you know there is wind, when you watch a hurricane tossing the waves about or tearing down homes; or when, in the soft evening breeze, it kisses the flowers and makes dewdrops hang in pearly coronets around the rose.

Have you ever seen electricity? No, but you know there is such a thing, for it travels along the wires for thousands of miles and carries our messages. Although you cannot see the thing itself, you know there is such a thing. In the same way, you must believe there is a Holy Spirit working in us, *"both to will and to do of his good pleasure"* (Phil. 2:13), even though it is beyond our senses.

THE WORLD DOES NOT KNOW HIM

Another reason why worldly men laugh at the doctrine of the Holy Spirit is because they do not know Him. If they knew Him through heartfelt experiences; if they recognized His work in their souls; if they had ever been touched by Him; if they had ever trembled under a sense of sin; if they had had their hearts melted, then they would never have doubted the existence of the Holy Spirit.

WORDS TO THE SAINTS

And now, beloved, our text says, *"He dwelleth with you, and shall be in you."* I will conclude with that sweet recollection—the Holy Spirit dwells in all believers and will be with them.

One word of comment and advice to the saints of God and to sinners, and I will be done. Saints of the Lord, you have heard that God the Holy Spirit is a person. You have had it proved to your souls. What should follow the understanding of this truth? Why, it follows how earnest you should be in prayer to the Holy Spirit, as well as for the Holy Spirit. You should lift up your prayers to the Holy Spirit. You should cry earnestly to Him, for He is *"able to do exceeding abundantly above all that we ask or think"* (Eph. 3:20).

Look at the mass of people in this church.* What is to convert it? See this crowd? Who is to make my influence permeate through the mass? You know this place now has a mighty influence, and, God blessing us, it will have an influence not only upon this city, but also upon England at large, for we now employ the printing press as well as the pulpit. Certainly, I should say, before the close of the year, more than two hundred thousand of my productions will be scattered through the land—words uttered by my lips or written by my pen.

But how can this influence be rendered for good? How will God's glory be promoted by it? Only by incessant prayer for the Holy Spirit, by constantly calling down the influence of the Holy Spirit upon us. We want Him to rest upon every page that is printed and upon every word that is uttered. Let us then be doubly earnest in pleading with the Holy Spirit that He would come and own our labors, that the whole church at large may be revived thereby. May not only ourselves share in the benefit, but also the whole world.

---

* Spurgeon delivered this message to the congregation at New Park Street Chapel, Southwark, a borough of London, England, on January 21, 1855.

WORDS TO THE SINNERS

To the ungodly, I have this one closing word to say. Ever be careful how you speak of the Holy Spirit. I do not know what the unpardonable sin is, and I do not think any man understands it, but it is something like this: "He who speaks a word against the Holy Spirit, it will never be forgiven him." I do not know what that means, but tread carefully!

There is danger. There is a pit that our ignorance has covered by sand. Tread carefully. You may be in it before the next hour! If there is any strife in your heart today, perhaps you will go to a barroom and forget it. Perhaps there is some voice speaking in your soul, and you will put it away. I do not know if you will be resisting the Holy Spirit and committing the unpardonable sin, but it is somewhere there.

Be very careful. There is no crime on earth as black as the crime against the Holy Spirit! You may blaspheme the Father, and you will be damned for it unless you repent. You may blaspheme the Son, and hell will be your portion unless you are forgiven. But blaspheme the Holy Spirit, and thus says the Lord:

All manner of sin and blasphemy shall be forgiven unto men: but the blasphemy against the Holy Ghost shall not be forgiven unto men. And whosoever speaketh a word against the Son of man, it shall be forgiven him: but whosoever speaketh against the Holy Ghost, it shall not be forgiven him, neither in this world, neither in the world to come.

(Matt. 12:31–32)

I cannot tell you what it is. I do not profess to understand it, but there it is. It is the danger signal:

Stop, man, stop! If you have despised the Holy Spirit, if you have laughed at His revelations and scorned what Christians call His influence, I beg you, stop! Take time right now to deliberate seriously. Perhaps some of you have actually committed the unpardonable sin; stop! Let fear stop you; sit down. Do not drive on so rashly as you have done, Jehu! (See 2 Kings 9:20.) Oh, slacken your reins! You who are such a profligate in sin, you who have uttered such hard words against the Trinity, stop! Ah, this warning makes us all stop! It makes us all draw up, and say, "Have I perhaps done so?" Let us think of this; and let us not at any time stifle the Holy Spirit of God either with our words or actions.

Chapter 5

The Intercession of the Holy Spirit

*Likewise the Spirit also helpeth our infirmities: for
we know not what we should pray for as we ought:
but the Spirit itself maketh intercession for us with
groanings which cannot be uttered. And he that
searcheth the hearts knoweth what is the mind of the
Spirit, because he maketh intercession for the saints
according to the will of God.*
—Romans 8:26–27

The apostle Paul wrote to a tried and afflicted
people, and one of his purposes was to remind
them of the rivers of comfort that were flowing near
at hand.

RIVERS OF COMFORT

THE COMFORT OF SONSHIP

First of all, he stirred up their pure minds by
reminding them of their sonship, for he said, *"As
many as are led by the Spirit of God, they are the sons
of God"* (Rom. 8:14). They were, therefore, encour-
aged to side with Christ, the elder brother, with
whom they had become *"joint-heirs"* (v. 17). They

were exhorted to *"suffer with him"* (v. 17) so that afterward they might be glorified with Him. All that they endured came from the Father's hand, and this should comfort them. A thousand sources of joy are opened in that one blessing of adoption. *"Blessed be the God and Father of our Lord Jesus Christ"* (1 Pet. 1:3), by whom we have been begotten into the family of grace (vv. 3–4).

THE COMFORT OF HOPE

After Paul had alluded to that consoling subject, he turned to the next ground of comfort, namely, that we are to be sustained during our present trials by hope. There is an amazing glory reserved for us, and though as yet we cannot enter into it, but in harmony with the whole creation must continue to groan and travail (Rom. 8:22), yet the hope of this itself should minister strength to us, and enable us patiently to bear *"our light affliction, which is but for a moment"* (2 Cor. 4:17).

This truth is full of sacred refreshment: hope sees a crown in reserve (2 Tim. 4:8), mansions in readiness, and Jesus Himself preparing a place for us (John 14:2), and by this rapturous sight, hope sustains the soul under the sorrows of the hour. Hope is the grand anchor by whose means we ride out the present storm.

THE COMFORT OF HIS ABIDING PRESENCE

The apostle then turned to a third source of comfort, namely, the abiding of the Holy Spirit in and with the Lord's people. He used the word *"likewise"* to intimate that in the same manner as hope sustains the soul, the Holy Spirit strengthens us under trial. Hope operates spiritually upon our spiritual faculties, and so does the Holy Spirit. In some mysterious way, He divinely operates upon the newborn faculties of the believer, so that he is sustained under his infirmities. In His light, we will see light. I pray, therefore, that we may be helped by the Spirit while we consider His mysterious operations so that we may not fall into error or miss precious truths through the blindness of our hearts.

The text speaks of *"our infirmities,"* or—as many translators put it in the singular—of "our infirmity." By this is meant our affliction and the weakness that trouble reveals in us. The Holy Spirit helps us to bear the infirmity of our bodies and of our minds; He helps us to bear our cross, whether it is physical pain, mental depression, spiritual conflict, slander, poverty, or persecution. He helps our infirmity, and with a Helper so divinely strong, we do not need to fear the result. God's grace will be sufficient for us; His *"strength is made perfect in weakness"* (2 Cor. 12:9).

I think, dear friends, you will all admit that if a man can pray, his troubles are at once lightened. When we feel that we have power with God and can obtain anything we ask for from His hands, then our difficulties cease to oppress us. We take our burdens to our heavenly Father and express them in the accents of childlike confidence; we come away quite content to bear whatever His holy will may lay upon us.

Prayer is a great outlet for grief; it draws up the sluices and abates the swelling flood that otherwise might be too strong for us. We bathe our wounds in the lotion of prayer, and the pain is lulled, the fever removed. Our minds may become so disturbed and our hearts so perplexed that we do not know how to pray. We see the mercy seat, and we perceive that God will hear us. We have no doubt about that, for we know that we are His own favored children, yet we hardly know what to desire. We fall into such heaviness of spirit and complexity of thought that the one remedy of prayer, which we have always found to be unfailing, appears to be taken from us. Here, then, in the nick of time, as *"a very present help in trouble"* (Ps. 46:1), comes the Holy Spirit. He draws near to teach us how to pray, and in this way He helps our infirmity, relieves our suffering, and enables us to bear the heavy burden without fainting under the load.

At this time, let us consider, first, the help that the Holy Spirit gives; second, the prayers that He inspires; and third, the success that such prayers are certain to obtain.

The Help the Holy Spirit Gives

First, the help that the Holy Spirit gives meets the weakness that we deplore. If in times of trouble a man can pray, his burden loses its weight. If the believer can take anything and everything to God, then he learns to glory in infirmities (2 Cor. 12:9) and to rejoice in tribulation, but sometimes we are in such confusion of mind that *"we know not what we should pray for as we ought."*

Knowing What to Pray For

In a measure, through our ignorance, we never know what we should pray for until we are taught by the Spirit of God, but there are times when this beclouding of the soul is dense indeed, and we do not even know what would help us out of our trouble if we could obtain it.

The Holy Spirit sees the disease, but we do not even know the name of the medicine we need. We look over the many things that we might ask for from the Lord, and we feel that each of them would be helpful, but that none of them would precisely meet our case. We could ask with confidence for spiritual blessings that we know to be according to the divine will, but perhaps these would not meet our specific circumstances. There are other things for which we are allowed to ask, but we scarcely know whether, if we had them, they would really meet our needs, and we also feel a reluctance to pray for them.

In praying for temporal things, we plead with measured voices, ever referring our petition for revision to the will of the Lord. Moses was not permitted to enter Canaan, for God denied him. (See Numbers 20:8–12; Deuteronomy 34:4.) The man who was healed begged the Lord to be able to go with Him, but Jesus gave him this answer, *"Go home to* [your] *friends"* (Mark 5:19 NKJV). Regarding future events, we pray about such matters with this reserve, "Nevertheless, not what I want, but as You desire." (See Matthew 26:39.) At times this very spirit of resignation appears to increase our spiritual difficulty, for we do not wish to ask for anything that would be contrary to the mind of God, and yet we must ask for something. We are reduced to such straits that we must pray, but what will be the particular subject of prayer we cannot for a while make out. Even when ignorance and perplexity are removed, we still do not know *"what we should pray for as we ought."*

HOW TO PRAY

When we know the matter of prayer, we often fail to pray in the right manner. We ask, but we are afraid that we will not receive, because we do not exercise the thought or the faith that we judge to be essential to prayer. At times, we cannot command the earnestness that is the life of supplication. A lethargy steals over us, our heart is chilled, our hand is numbed, and we cannot wrestle with the angel. (See Genesis 32:24–29.)

We know what material objects to pray for, but we do not know what to pray for *"as we ought."* It is the manner of the prayer that perplexes us, even when the matter is decided upon. How can I pray? My mind wanders; I trumpet like a whooping crane; I roar like a beast in pain; I moan in the brokenness of my heart, but, oh, I do not know what it is my inmost spirit needs. Or, if I know it, I do not know how to frame my petition properly before Him. I do not know how to open my lips in His majestic presence. I am so troubled that I cannot speak. My spiritual distress robs me of the power to pour out my heart before my God. Now, beloved, it is in such a plight as this that the Holy Spirit aids us with His divine help. Hence, He is *"a very present help in trouble"* (Ps. 46:1).

INSTRUCTION

Coming to our aid in our bewilderment, He instructs us. This is one of His frequent operations upon the mind of the believer: *"He will teach you all things"* (John 14:26 NKJV). He instructs us as to our need, and as to the promises of God that refer to that need. He shows us where our deficiencies are, what our sins are, and what our needs are. He sheds a light on our condition and makes us feel deeply our helplessness, sinfulness, and dire poverty. Then He casts the same light upon the promises of the Word and lays home to the heart that very text that was intended to meet the occasion—the precise promise that was framed with the foresight of our present distress. In that light He makes the promise shine in all its truthfulness, certainty, sweetness, and suitability, so that we, poor trembling sons of men, dare to take that Word into our mouths that first came out of God's mouth, and then come with it as an argument and plead it before the throne of the heavenly grace. Our power in prayer lies in the plea, "Lord, do as You have said."

How greatly we ought to value the Holy Spirit, because when we are in the dark, He gives us light, and when our perplexed spirit is so befogged and beclouded that it cannot see its own need, and cannot find the appropriate promise in the Scriptures, the Spirit of God comes in, teaches us all things, and brings to our remembrance everything that our Lord has told us (John 14:26).

GUIDANCE

He guides us in prayer; thus, He helps our infirmities. But the blessed Spirit does more than this; He will often direct the mind to the special subject of prayer. He dwells within us as our Counselor and points out to us what it is we should seek at the hands of God. We do not know why it is so, but we sometimes find our minds carried as by a strong undercurrent into a particular line of prayer for some definite purpose. It is not merely that our judgment leads us in that direction, though usually the Spirit of God acts upon us by enlightening our judgment, but we often feel an unaccountable and irresistible desire rising within our hearts. This so presses upon us that we not only utter the desire before God at our ordinary times for prayer, but also feel it crying in our hearts all the day long, almost to the supplanting of all other considerations. At such times we should thank God for direction and give our desire a clear road: the Holy Spirit is granting us inward direction as to how we can count on good success in our pleadings. The Spirit will give such guidance to each of you if you will ask Him to illuminate you.

He will guide you both negatively and positively. Negatively, He will forbid you to pray for certain things, just as Paul tried *"to go into Bithynia: but the Spirit suffered* [him] *not"* (Acts 16:7). On the other hand, He will cause you to hear a cry within your soul that will guide your petitions, even as He made Paul to hear the cry from Macedonia, saying, *"Come over into Macedonia, and help us"* (v. 9).

The Spirit teaches wisely, as no other teacher can do. Those who obey His promptings will not walk in darkness. He leads the spiritual eye to take good and steady aim at the very center of the target, and thus we hit the mark in our pleadings.

INTERCESSION

Nor is this all, for the Spirit of God is not sent merely to guide and help our devotion, but He *"maketh intercession for the saints according to the will of God."* This expression does not mean that the Holy Spirit groans or personally prays, but that He excites intense desire and creates inexpressible groanings in us, and these are ascribed to Him. Solomon built the temple because he superintended and ordained it all, yet I do not know that he ever fashioned a timber or prepared a stone. Likewise, the Holy Spirit prays and pleads within us by leading us to pray and plead. This He does by arousing our desires.

The Holy Spirit has a wonderful power over renewed hearts, as much power as the skillful musician has over the strings on which he lays his experienced hand. The influences of the Holy Spirit at times pass through the soul like winds through an aeolian harp, creating and inspiring sweet notes of gratitude and tones of desire, to which we would have been strangers if it had not been for His divine visitation.

He can arouse us from our lethargy, He can warm us out of our lukewarmness, and He can enable us when we are on our knees to rise above the ordinary routine of prayer into that victorious importunity against which nothing can stand. He can lay certain desires so pressingly upon our hearts that we can never rest until they are fulfilled. He can make the zeal for God's house to eat us up (Ps. 69:9; John 2:17), and the passion for God's glory to be like *"a burning fire shut up in* [our] *bones"* (Jer. 20:9); inspiring our prayers is one part of that process by which He helps our infirmity. True Advocate is He, and Comforter most effectual. Blessed be His name.

STRENGTH

The Holy Spirit also divinely operates in the strengthening of the faith of believers. At first, that faith is of His creating, and afterward, it is of His sustaining and increasing. Oh, brothers and sisters, have you not often felt your faith rise in proportion to your trials? Have you not, like Noah's ark, mounted toward heaven as the flood deepened around you? You have felt as sure about the promise as you felt about the trial. The affliction was, as it were, in your very bones, but the promise was also in your heart. You could not doubt the affliction, for you smarted under it, but you also could not doubt the divine help, for your confidence was firm and unmoved.

Only the greatest faith is what God has a right to expect from us, yet we never exhibit it unless the Holy Spirit strengthens our confidence and opens up before us the covenant with all its seals and securities. It is He who leads our soul to cry, *"Although my house be not so with God; yet he hath made with me an everlasting covenant, ordered in all things, and sure"* (2 Sam. 23:5). Blessed be the divine Spirit then, that since faith is essential to prevailing prayer, He helps us in supplication by increasing our faith. Without faith, prayer cannot speed, for he who wavers *"is like a wave of the sea driven with the wind and tossed"* (James 1:6), and such a person may not expect *"any thing of the Lord"* (v. 7); happy are we when the Holy Spirit removes our wavering and enables us like Abraham to believe without staggering, knowing full well that He who has promised is *"able also to perform"* (Rom. 4:20–21). Using three examples, I will endeavor to describe the work of the Spirit of God in this matter, though they all fall short, and indeed all that I can say must fall infinitely short of the glory of His work. The actual mode of His working upon the mind we may not attempt to explain; it remains a mystery, and it would be an unholy intrusion to attempt to remove the veil. There is no difficulty in our believing that as one human mind operates upon another mind, so does the Holy Spirit influence our spirits. We are forced to use words if we would influence our fellowmen, but the Spirit of God can operate upon the human mind more directly and communicate with it in silence. Into that matter, however, we will not dive lest we intrude where our knowledge would be drowned by our presumption.

LIKE A PROMPTER

My illustrations do not touch the mystery, but set forth the grace. The Holy Spirit acts to His people somewhat as a prompter to a reciter. A man has to deliver a piece that he has learned, but his memory is treacherous. Therefore, somewhere out of sight, there is a prompter, so that when the speaker is at a loss and might use a wrong word, a whisper is heard that suggests the right one. When the speaker has almost lost the thread of his speech, he turns his ear, and the prompter gives him the word and aids his memory. If I may be allowed the simile, I would say that this represents in part the work of the Spirit of God in us, suggesting to us the right desire, and bringing all things to our remembrance, whatever Christ has told us (John 14:26).

In prayer we would often come to a dead end, but He incites, suggests, inspires, and so we go forward. In prayer we might grow weary, but the Comforter encourages and refreshes us with encouraging thoughts. When we are in our bewilderment almost driven to give up prayer, the whisper of His love drops a live coal from off the altar into our soul, and our hearts glow with greater ardor than before. Regard the Holy Spirit as your prompter, and let your ears be opened to His voice. But He is much more than this.

LIKE AN ADVOCATE

Let me attempt a second simile: the Holy Spirit is like an advocate to one in peril with the law. Suppose that a poor man had a great lawsuit concerning his whole estate, and he was forced personally to go into court to plead his own cause and speak up for his rights. If he were an uneducated man, he would be in a poor plight. An adversary in the court might plead against him and overthrow him, for he could not answer him. This poor man knows very little about the law and is quite unable to meet his cunning opponent.

Suppose one who was perfect in the law would take up his cause warmly and come and live with him. He would use all his knowledge so as to prepare his case for him, draw up his petitions, and fill his mouth with arguments. Would that not be a grand relief?

This counselor would suggest the line of pleading, arrange the arguments, and put them into proper legal language. When the poor man was baffled by a question asked in court, he would run home and ask his adviser. His friend would tell him exactly how to meet the objector. Suppose, too, that when he had to plead with the judge himself, this advocate at home would teach him how to behave and what to present, and encourage him to hope that he would prevail. Would this not be a great blessing?

Who would be the pleader in such a case? The poor client would plead, but still, when he won the suit, he would trace it all to the advocate who lived at his home and gave him counsel. Indeed, it would be the advocate pleading for him, even while he pleaded himself. This is an instructive symbol of a great fact. Within this narrow house of my body, this tenement of clay, if I am a true believer, the Holy Spirit dwells there, and when I desire to pray, I may ask Him what I should pray for as I ought, and He will help me. He will write the prayers that I ought to offer upon the tablets of my heart, and I will see them there, and so I will be taught how to plead. It will be the Spirit's own Self pleading in me, and by me, and through me, before the throne of grace. What a happy man in his lawsuit would such a poor man be, and how happy are you and I that we have the Holy Spirit to be our Counselor!

LIKE A FATHER

Yet one more illustration. It is that of a father helping his son. Suppose it is a time of war centuries ago. Old English warfare to a great extent was then conducted by bowmen. Here is a youth who is to be initiated in the art of archery; therefore, he carries a bow. It is a strong bow and very hard to draw; indeed, it requires more strength than the youth can summon to bend it.

See how his father teaches him. "Put your right hand here, my boy, and place your left hand so. Now pull." As the youth pulls back, his father's hands are on the boy's hands, and the bow is drawn. The lad draws the bow, but it is quite as much his father's strength that is pulling the bow as it is the boy's.

We cannot draw the bow of prayer alone. Sometimes a bow of steel is not broken by our hands, for we cannot even bend it. Then the Holy Spirit puts His mighty hand over ours and covers our weakness so that we draw; and then, what a splendid drawing of the bow it is! The bow bends so easily we wonder how that could be. Away flies the arrow, and it pierces the very center of the target, for He who gives has won the day, but it was His secret might that made us strong, and to Him be the glory of it. Thus have I tried to set forth the encouraging fact that the Spirit helps the people of God.

THE PRAYER THE HOLY SPIRIT INSPIRES

Our second subject is that part of prayer that is especially and distinctively the work of the Spirit of God. The text says, *"The Spirit itself maketh intercession for us with groanings which cannot be uttered."* It is not the Spirit who groans, but we who groan; however, as I have shown you, the Spirit excites the emotion that causes us to groan. It is clear, then, that the prayers that are composed in us by the Spirit of God are those that arise from our inmost soul. A man's heart is moved when he groans.

A groan is a matter about which there is no hypocrisy. A groan comes not from the lips, but from the heart. A groan, then, is a part of prayer that we owe to the Holy Spirit, and the same is true of all the prayer that wells up from the deep fountains of our inner lives. The prophet Jeremiah cried, *"My bowels, my bowels! I am pained at my very heart; my heart maketh a noise in me"* (Jer. 4:19). This deep ground swell of desire, this tidal motion of the life-floods, is caused by the Holy Spirit. His work is never superficial, but always deep and inward.

PRAYERS OF ANGUISH

Such prayers will rise within us when the mind is far too troubled to let us speak. We do not know *"what we should pray for as we ought,"* and it is then that we groan or utter some other inarticulate sound. Hezekiah said, *"Like a crane or a swallow, so did I chatter"* (Isa. 38:14). The psalmist said, *"I am so troubled that I cannot speak"* (Ps. 77:4), and *"I have roared by reason of the disquietness of my heart"* (Ps. 38:8); but he added, *"Lord, all my desire is before thee; and my groaning is not hid from thee"* (v. 9). The sighing of the prisoner surely comes up into the ears of the Lord. There is real prayer in these *"groanings which cannot be uttered."*

It is the power of the Holy Spirit in us that creates all real prayer, even that which takes the form of a groan because the mind is incapable, by reason of its bewilderment and grief, of clothing its emotion in words. I pray that you will never think lightly of the supplications of your anguish. Rather, judge that such prayers are like Jabez, of whom it is written, *"And Jabez was more honourable than his brethren: and his mother called his name Jabez, saying, Because I bare him with sorrow"* (1 Chron. 4:9). What is brought forth from the depth of the soul, when it is stirred with a terrible tempest, is more precious than pearl or coral, for it is the intercession of the Holy Spirit.

PRAYERS EXPRESSING GREAT NEED

These prayers are sometimes *"groanings which cannot be uttered,"* because they concern such great things that they cannot be spoken. I am in need, my Lord! I need, I need. I cannot tell you what I need, but I seem to need so many things. If it were just a little thing, my narrow capacity could comprehend and describe it, but I need all Your covenant blessings. You know what I need before I ask You (Matt. 6:8), and although I cannot explain each item of my need, I know it to be very great, and more than I myself can ever estimate.

I groan, for I can do no more. Prayers that are the offspring of great desires, sublime aspirations, and elevated designs are surely the work of the Holy Spirit, and their power within a man is frequently so great that he cannot find expression for them. Words fail, and even the sighs that try to embody them cannot be uttered.

INARTICULATE PRAYERS

It may be, beloved, that we groan because we are conscious of the littleness of our desires and of the narrowness of our faith. The trial itself may seem too insignificant to pray about. I have known what it is to feel as if I could not pray about a certain matter, and yet I have been obliged to groan about it. A *"thorn in the flesh"* (2 Cor. 12:7) may be as painful a thing as a sword in the bones, and yet we may go and beseech the Lord three times about it (see verse 8), and getting no answer we may feel that *"we know not what we should pray for as we ought,"* and yet it makes us groan. Yes, and with that natural groan there may go up an unutterable groaning of the Holy Spirit.

Beloved, what a different view of prayer God has from what men think to be the correct one. You may have seen very beautiful prayers in print, and you may have heard very charming compositions from the pulpit, but I trust you have not fallen in love with the sound of them. Judge these things rightly. I pray that you will never think well of fine prayers, for before the thrice-holy God, it is unbecoming for a sinful suppliant to play the orator.

We have heard of a certain clergyman who was said to have prayed "the finest prayer ever offered to a Boston audience." Just so! The Boston audience received the prayer, and there it ended. We want the mind of the Spirit in prayer, and not the mind of the flesh. (See Romans 8:5.) The tail feathers of pride should be pulled out of our prayers, for they need only the wing feathers of faith. The peacock feathers of poetical expression are out of place before the throne of God. Someone says, "What remarkably beautiful language he used in prayer! What an intellectual treat his prayer was!" Yes, yes, but God looks at the heart (1 Sam. 16:7). To Him, fine language is *"as sounding brass, or a tinkling cymbal"* (1 Cor. 13:1), but a groan has music in it.

We do not like groans. Our ears are much too delicate to tolerate such dreary sounds, but not so the great Father of spirits. A Methodist brother cries, "Amen," and you say, "I cannot bear such

Methodistic noise." No, but if it comes from the man's heart, God can bear it. When you go upstairs to your room this evening to pray and find you cannot pray, but have to moan, "Lord, I am too full of anguish and too perplexed to pray; hear the voice of my roaring," though you reach to nothing else, you will be really praying. When we can say like David, *"I opened my mouth, and panted"* (Ps. 119:131), we are by no means in a bad state of mind.

All flowery language in prayer, and especially all intoning or performing of prayers, must be abhorrent to God; it is little short of profanity to offer solemn supplication to God after the manner called "intoning." The sighing of a true heart is infinitely more acceptable, for it is the work of the Spirit of God.

PRAYERS OF KNOWLEDGE

We may say of the prayers that the Holy Spirit works in us that they are prayers of knowledge. Notice, our difficulty is that we do not know what we should pray for, but the Holy Spirit does know; therefore, He helps us by enabling us to pray intelligently, knowing what we are asking for, so far as this knowledge is needful to valid prayer. The text speaks of *"the mind of the Spirit."* What a mind that must be! It is the mind of the Spirit who arranged all the order that now pervades this earth! There once was chaos and confusion, but the Holy Spirit brooded over all, and His mind is the originator of that beautiful arrangement that we so admire in the visible creation. What a mind this must be!

The Holy Spirit's mind is seen in our intercessions when under His sacred influence we present our cases before the Lord and plead with holy wisdom for things convenient and necessary. What wise and admirable desires must those be that the Spirit of Wisdom Himself works in us!

ACCEPTABLE PRAYERS

Moreover, the Holy Spirit's intercession creates prayers offered in a proper manner. I showed you that the difficulty is that *"we know not what we should pray for as we ought,"* and the Spirit meets that difficulty by making intercession for us in a right manner. The Holy Spirit works in us humility, earnestness, intensity, importunity, faith, resignation, and all else that is acceptable to God in our supplications. We do not know how to mingle these sacred spices in the incense of prayer. If left to ourselves, at our very best, we get too much of one ingredient or another and spoil the sacred compound, but the Holy Spirit's intercessions have in them such a blessed blending of all that is good that they come up as a sweet perfume before the Lord.

Spirit-taught prayers are offered as they ought to be. They are His own intercession in some respects, for we read that the Holy Spirit not only helps us to intercede but also *"maketh intercession."* It is stated twice in our text that He *"maketh intercession for us."* I tried to show the meaning of this when I described a father putting his hands upon his child's hands. This is something more than helping us to pray, something more than encouraging us or directing us, but I venture no further, except to say that He puts such force of His own mind into our poor weak thoughts and desires and hopes that He

Himself *"maketh intercession for us,"* working in us to will and to pray according to *"his good pleasure"* (Phil. 2:13).

PRAYERS FOR THE SAINTS

Notice, however, that these intercessions of the Spirit are only in the saints. *"The Spirit...maketh intercession for us,"* and *"He maketh intercession for the saints."* Does He do nothing for sinners then? Yes, He quickens sinners into spiritual life, and He strives with them to overcome their sinfulness and turn them into the right way; but in the saints, He works with us and enables us to pray after His mind and according to the will of God.

His intercession is not in or for the unregenerate. Oh, unbelievers, you must first be made saints, or you cannot feel the Spirit's intercession within you. What need we have to go to Christ for the blessing of the Holy Spirit. It can be ours only by faith in Christ Jesus! *"But as many as received him, to them gave he power to become the sons of God"* (John 1:12). *"The Spirit of adoption"* (Rom. 8:15) and all His helping grace comes to the children of God alone. Unless we are the children of God, the Holy Spirit's indwelling will not be ours. We are shut out from the intercession of the Holy Spirit and from the intercession of Jesus, too, for He has said, *"I pray not for the world, but for them which thou hast given me"* (John 17:9). Thus I have tried to show you the kind of prayers that the Spirit inspires.

THE SURE SUCCESS OF INSPIRED PRAYERS

Our third and last point is that all of the prayers that the Spirit of God inspires in us must succeed.

GOD UNDERSTANDS OUR PRAYERS

First, there is a meaning in our prayers that God reads and approves. When the Spirit of God writes a prayer upon a man's heart, the man himself may be in such a state of mind that he does not altogether know what it is. His interpretation of it is a groan, and that is all. Perhaps he does not even get so far as that in expressing the mind of the Spirit, but he feels *"groanings which cannot be uttered."* He cannot find a door of utterance for his inward grief.

Yet our heavenly Father, who looks immediately upon the heart, reads what the Spirit of God has written there and does not need even our groans to explain the meaning. He reads the heart itself. He *"knoweth,"* says the text, *"what is the mind of the Spirit."* The Spirit is one with the Father, and the Father knows what the Spirit means.

The desires that the Spirit prompts may be too spiritual for such babes in grace as we are to actually describe or express, yet the Spirit writes the desire on the renewed mind, and the Father sees it. Now what God reads in the heart and approves of—for the word *"knoweth"* in this case includes approval as well as the act of omniscience—what God sees and approves of in the heart must succeed. Did not Jesus say, *"Your heavenly Father knoweth that ye have need of all these things"* (Matt. 6:32)? Did He not tell us this as an encouragement to believe that we will receive all necessary blessings? So it is with those prayers that are all broken up, wet with tears, and discordant with those sighs and inarticulate expressions, heavings of the chest and sobbings of the heart, and anguish and bitterness of spirit. Our gracious Lord reads them as a man reads a book, and they are written in a character that He fully understands.

To give a simple example: if I were to come into your house I might find a little child there who cannot yet speak plainly. He cries for something, and he makes very odd and objectionable noises, combined with signs and movements, which are almost meaningless to a stranger, but his mother understands him and attends to his little pleadings. A mother can translate baby talk. She comprehends incomprehensible noises. Even so does our Father in heaven know all about our poor baby talk, for our prayers are not much better. He knows and comprehends the cryings, meanings, sighings, and chatterings of His bewildered children. Yes, a tender mother knows her child's needs before the child knows what he wants. Perhaps the little one stutters, stammers, and cannot get his words out, but the mother sees what he would say and understands the meaning. Likewise, we know concerning our great Father:

> He knows the thoughts we mean to speak,
> Ere from our opening lips they break.

Rejoice in this, because the prayers of the Spirit are known and understood of God; therefore, they will be sure to succeed.

GOD AGREES WITH PRAYERS PROMPTED BY THE HOLY SPIRIT

The next argument for making us sure that our prayers will go forth is this: they are *"the mind of the Spirit."* God the Ever Blessed is one, and there can be no division among the Father, the Son, and the Holy Spirit. These Divine Persons always work together. There is a common desire for the glory of each blessed person of the Divine Trinity; therefore, it cannot be conceived, without being profane, that anything could be the mind of the Holy Spirit and not be the mind of the Father and the mind of the Son as well.

The mind of God is one and harmonious; if, therefore, the Holy Spirit dwells in you, and He moves you to any desire, then His mind is in your prayers, and it is not possible that the eternal Father would reject your petitions. The prayer that came from heaven will certainly go back to heaven. If the Holy Spirit prompts it, the Father must and will accept it, for it is not possible that He would slight the ever blessed and adorable Spirit.

PRAYERS FROM THE SPIRIT ARE ACCORDING TO THE WILL OF GOD

One more word completes the argument, namely, that the work of the Spirit in the heart is not only *"the mind of the Spirit"* that God knows, but it is also according to the will or mind of God, for the Holy Spirit never makes intercession in us other than is consistent with the divine will.

Now, the divine will or mind may be viewed in two ways. First, there is the will declared in the proclamations of holiness in the Ten Commandments. The Spirit of God never prompts us to ask for anything that is unholy or inconsistent with the precepts of the Lord. Second, there is the secret mind of God, the will of His eternal predestination and decree, of which we know nothing; but we do know this, that the Spirit of God never prompts us to ask anything that is contrary to the eternal purpose of God.

Reflect for a moment: the Holy Spirit knows all the purposes of God, and when they are about to be fulfilled, He moves the children of God to pray about them, and so their prayers keep touch and tally with the divine decrees. Oh, would you not pray confidently if you knew that your prayers corresponded with the sealed book of destiny? We may safely entreat the Lord to do what He has ordained to do.

A carnal man draws the inference that if God has ordained an event, we need not pray about it, but faith obediently draws the inference that the God who secretly ordained to give the blessing has openly commanded that we should pray for it, and therefore, faith obediently prays.

Coming events cast their shadows before them, and when God is about to bless His people, His coming favor casts the shadow of prayer over the church. When He is about to favor an individual, He casts the shadow of hopeful expectation over his soul. Let men laugh at our prayers as they will, and say there is no power in them. They are the indicators of the movement of the wheels of Providence.

Believing supplications are forecasts of the future. He who prays in faith is like the seer of old; he sees what is to be. His holy expectancy, like a telescope, brings distant objects near to him. He is bold to declare that he has the petition that he has asked of God, and he therefore begins to rejoice and to praise God, even before the blessing has actually arrived. So it is: prayer prompted by the Holy Spirit is the footfall of the divine decree.

I conclude by saying, my dear friends, see the absolute necessity of the Holy Spirit, for if the saints *"know not what* [they] *should pray for as* [they] *ought,"* if consecrated men and women, with Christ suffering in them, still feel their need of the instruction of the Holy Spirit, how much more do you who are not saints, and have never given yourselves up to God, require divine teaching! Oh, that you would know and feel your dependence upon the Holy Spirit so that He may prompt the once crucified but now ascended Redeemer, so that this gift of the Spirit, this promise of the Father, may be shed abroad upon men.

May He who comes from Jesus lead you to Jesus. And then, people of God, let this last thought stay with you: what condescension that the Divine Person would dwell in you forever, and that He would be with you to help your prayers! Listen to me for a moment. If I read in the Scriptures that in the most heroic acts of faith, God the Holy Spirit helps His people, I can understand it; if I read that in the sweetest music of their songs when they worship best and chant their loftiest strains before the Most High God, the Spirit helps them, I can understand it; and even if I hear that in their wrestling prayers and prevalent intercessions, God the Holy Spirit helps them, I can understand it: but I bow with reverent amazement, my heart sinking into the dust with adoration, when I reflect that God the Holy Spirit helps us when we cannot speak, but only groan. Yes, and when we cannot even utter our groanings, He not only helps us but also claims as His own particular creation the *"groanings which cannot be uttered."* This is condescension indeed!

In deigning to help us in the grief that cannot even vent itself in groaning, He proves Himself to be a true Comforter. "O God, my God, You have not forsaken me. You are not far from me or from the voice of my roaring. (See Psalm 22:1.) You left the Firstborn for a while when He was made a curse for us, so that He cried in agony, *'Why hast thou forsaken me?'* (Matt. 27:46), but You will not leave one of the *'many brethren'* (Rom. 8:29) for whom He died. The Spirit will be with them, and when they cannot so much as groan, He will make intercession for them with *'groanings which cannot be uttered.'"*

God bless you, my beloved brethren, and may you feel the Spirit of the Lord working in you and with you.

Chapter 6

Adoption—The Spirit and the Cry

And because ye are sons, God hath sent forth
the Spirit of his Son into your hearts,
crying, Abba, Father.
—Galatians 4:6

We do not find the doctrine of the unity of the Trinity set forth in Scripture in formal terms, such as those employed in the Athanasian Creed, which states, in part, "We worship one God in Trinity, and Unity....The Father is God, the Son God: and the Holy Ghost is God. And yet they are not three Gods: but one God."

But the truth of the triune God is continually taken for granted, as if it were a well-known fact in the church of God. If not expressed very often, in so many words, it is everywhere held in truth. It is mentioned incidentally, in connection with other truths, in a way that renders it quite as distinct as if it were expressed in a set formula. In many passages it is brought before us so prominently that we must be willfully blind if we do not see it.

In our text, for instance, we have distinct mention of each of the three Divine Persons. *"God,"* that is the Father, *"sent forth the Spirit,"* that is the Holy Spirit; and He is here called *"the Spirit of his Son."*

Nor have we the names alone, for each sacred person is mentioned as acting in the work of our salvation: *"God sent forth his Son"* (Gal. 4:4). Then note the fifth verse, which speaks of the Son as redeeming those who were under the law; and then the text itself reveals the Spirit as coming into the hearts of believers, and *"crying, Abba, Father."* Inasmuch as you have not only the mention of the separate names, but also certain special operations ascribed to each, it is plain that you have here the distinct personality of each.

Neither the Father, the Son, nor the Spirit can be an influence, or a mere form of existence, for each one acts in a divine manner, but with a special sphere and a distinct mode of operation. The error of regarding a certain Divine Person as a mere influence, or emanation, mainly assails the Holy Spirit; but its falseness is seen in the words, *"crying, Abba, Father."* An influence cannot cry; the act requires a person to perform it.

Though we may not understand the wonderful truth of the undivided unity and the distinct personality of the triune Godhead, nevertheless, we see this truth revealed in the Holy Scriptures; therefore, we accept it as a matter of faith.

The divinity of each of these sacred persons is also to be gathered from the text and its connection. We do not doubt the loving union of all in the work of deliverance. We reverence the Father, without whom we would not have been chosen or adopted.

Blessed be the God and Father of our Lord Jesus Christ, which according to his abundant mercy hath begotten us again unto a lively hope by the resurrection of Jesus Christ from the dead. (1 Pet. 1:3)

We love and reverence the Son by whose most precious blood we have been redeemed, and with whom we are one in a mystical and everlasting union. We adore and love the divine Spirit, for it is by Him that we have been regenerated, illuminated, quickened, preserved, and sanctified; and it is through Him that we receive the seal and witness within our hearts by which we are assured that we are indeed the sons of God.

God said, *"Let us make man in our image, after our likeness"* (Gen. 1:26). Even so do the Divine Persons take counsel together, and all unite in the new creation of the believer. We must not fail to bless, adore, and love each one of the exalted persons, but we must diligently bow in lowliest reverence before the one God—Father, Son, and Holy Spirit.

> Glory be to the Father,
> And to the Son,
> And to the Holy Spirit;
> As it was in the beginning,
> Is now, and ever will be,
> World without end. Amen.

Having noted this most important fact, let us come to the text itself, hoping to enjoy the doctrine of the Trinity while we are talking about our adoption, this wonder of grace in which They each have a share. Under the teaching of the Divine Spirit may we be drawn into sweet communion with the Father through His Son Jesus Christ, to His glory and to our benefit.

Three things are very clearly set forth in the text. The first is the dignity of believers—*"Ye are sons."* The second is the consequent indwelling of the Holy Spirit—*"Because ye are sons, God hath sent forth the Spirit of his Son into your hearts."* The third is the filial cry—*"crying, Abba, Father."*

THE DIGNITY OF BELIEVERS

First, adoption gives us the rights of children, and regeneration gives us the nature of children. We are partakers of both of these, for we are sons. And let us observe that this sonship is a gift of grace received by faith. We are not the sons of God by nature in the sense meant here. We are in a sense *"the off-spring of God"* (Acts 17:29) by nature, but this is very different from the sonship described in the text, which is the peculiar privilege of those who are born again.

The Jews claimed to be of the family of God, but as their privileges came to them by way of their fleshly birth, they are likened to Ishmael, who was born after the flesh, but who was cast out as the son of the bondwoman and compelled to give way to the son of the promise. We have a sonship that does not come to us by nature, for we are *"born, not of blood, nor of the will of the flesh, nor of the will of man, but of God"* (John 1:13). Our sonship comes by promise, by the operation of God as a special gift to a peculiar seed, set apart unto the Lord by His own sovereign grace, as Isaac was. This honor and this privilege come to us by faith. Note well the twenty-sixth verse of the preceding chapter: *"For ye are all the children of God by faith in Christ Jesus"* (Gal. 3:26). As unbelievers we know nothing of adoption. While we are under the law, as self-righteous, we know something of servitude, but we know nothing of sonship. It is only after faith has come that we cease to be under the schoolmaster (vv. 24–25) and rise out of our minority to take the privileges of the sons of God.

JUSTIFICATION

Faith works in us the *"spirit of adoption"* (Rom. 8:15), and our consciousness of sonship, in this way: first, it brings us justification. Galatians 3:24 says, *"The law was our schoolmaster to bring us unto Christ, that we might be justified by faith."* An unjustified man stands in the condition of a criminal, not of a child. His sin is laid to his charge; he is reckoned as unjust and unrighteous, as indeed he really is; and he is therefore a rebel against his king, and not a child enjoying his father's love.

ADOPTION

But when faith realizes the cleansing power of the blood of the Atonement and lays hold of the righteousness of God in Christ Jesus, then the justified man becomes a son and a child. Justification and adoption always go together. *"Whom he called, them he also justified"* (Rom. 8:30), and the calling is a call to the Father's house and to a recognition of sonship. Believing brings forgiveness and justification through our Lord Jesus; it also brings adoption, for it is written, *"But as many as received him, to them gave he power to become the sons of God, even to them that believe on his name"* (John 1:12).

FREEDOM

In the next place, faith brings us into the realization of our adoption by setting us free from the bondage of the law. *"After that faith is come, we are no longer under a schoolmaster"* (Gal. 3:25). When we groaned under a sense of sin, and were shut up by it as in a prison, we feared that the law would punish us for our iniquity, and our life was made bitter with fear. Moreover, we strove in our own blind, self-sufficient manner to keep that law, and this brought us into yet another bondage, which became harder and harder as failure gave way to more failure. We sinned and stumbled more and more, to our soul's confusion.

SONSHIP

But now that faith has come, we see the law fulfilled in Christ, and ourselves justified and accepted in Him. This changes the slave into a child, and duty into choice. Now we delight in the law, and by the power of the Spirit, we walk in holiness to the glory of God. Thus it is that by believing in Christ Jesus, we escape from Moses, the taskmaster, and come to Jesus, the Savior. We cease to regard God as an angry Judge and view Him as our loving Father. The system of merit and command, punishment and fear, has given way to the rule of grace, gratitude, and love, and this new principle of government is one of the grand privileges of the children of God.

Now, faith is the mark of sonship in all who have it, whoever they may be, *"for ye are all the children of God by faith in Christ Jesus"* (Gal. 3:26). If you are believing in Jesus, whether you are a Jew or Gentile, bond or free, you are a son of God. If you have believed in Christ recently, and have only for the past few weeks been able to rest in His great salvation, even now, beloved, you are a child of God. It is not an after-privilege, granted to assurance or growth in grace; it is an early-blessing, and belongs to him who has the smallest degree of faith and is no more than a babe in grace. If a man is a believer in Jesus Christ, his name is in the registry of the great family above, *"for ye are all the children of God by faith in Christ Jesus."*

But if you have no faith, no matter what zeal, no matter what works, no matter what knowledge, no matter what pretensions to holiness you may possess, you are nothing, and your religion is vain. Without faith in Christ, you are *"as sounding brass, or a tinkling cymbal"* (1 Cor. 13:1), for *"without faith it is impossible to please* [God]*"* (Heb. 11:6). Faith then, wherever it is found, is the infallible token of a child of God, and its absence is fatal to the claim.

PUTTING ON CHRIST

This, according to the apostle Paul, is further illustrated by our baptism, for in baptism, if there is faith in the soul, there is an open "putting on" of the Lord Jesus Christ. *"For as many of you as have been baptized into Christ have put on Christ"* (Gal. 3:27). In baptism you professed to be dead to the world and you were therefore buried into the name of Jesus. The meaning of that burial, if it had any right meaning to you, was that you professed yourself henceforth to be dead to everything but Christ, and, from that point on, your life was to be in Him. You were to be as one *"raised up from the dead...*[to] *walk in newness of life"* (Rom. 6:4). Of course, the outward form avails nothing to the unbeliever, but to the one who is in Christ, it is a most instructive ordinance.

The spirit and essence of the law lie in the soul's entering into the symbol, in the man's knowing not only the baptism into water, but the baptism into the Holy Spirit and into fire. As many of you as know that inward mystical baptism into Christ know also that henceforth you have put on Christ and are covered by Him as a man is covered by his clothes. Henceforth you are one in Christ. You wear His name, you live in Him, you are saved by Him, and you are altogether His.

Now, if you are one with Christ, since He is the Son of God, you are sons also. If you have put on Christ, God sees you not in yourself but in Christ, and what belongs to Christ belongs also to you. *"If ye be Christ's, then are ye Abraham's seed, and heirs according to the promise"* (Gal. 3:29).

As the Roman youth put on the toga when he came of age, and was admitted to the rights of citizenship, so the putting on of Christ is the token of our admission into the position of sons of God. Thus are we actually admitted to the enjoyment of our glorious heritage. Every blessing of the covenant of grace belongs to those who are Christ's, and every believer is on that list. Thus, then, according to the teaching of the passage, we receive adoption by faith as the gift of grace.

REDEMPTION

Again, adoption comes to us by redemption. Read the passage that precedes the text:

But when the fulness of the time was come, God sent forth his Son, made of a woman, made under the law, to redeem them that were

> *under the law, that we might receive the adop-*
> *tion of sons.* (Gal. 4:4–5)

Beloved, prize redemption, and never listen to teaching that would destroy its meaning or lower its importance. Remember that you were not redeemed with *"silver and gold,…but with the precious blood of Christ, as of a lamb without blemish"* (1 Pet. 1:18–19).

You were under the law and subject to its curse, for you had broken it most grievously. You were subject to its penalty, for it is written, *"The soul who sins shall die"* (Ezek. 18:4 NKJV); and yet again, *"Cursed is everyone who does not continue in all things which are written in the book of the law, to do them"* (Gal. 3:10 NKJV).

You were also under the terror of the law, for you feared its wrath. You were under its irritating power, for often when the commandment came, sin within you revived, and you died (Rom. 7:9). But now you are redeemed from all. As the Holy Spirit says, *"Christ hath redeemed us from the curse of the law, being made a curse for us: for it is written, Cursed is every one that hangeth on a tree"* (Gal. 3:13). Now, you *"are not under the law, but under grace"* (Rom. 6:14), because Christ came under the law and kept it both by His active and His passive obedience, fulfilling all its commands and bearing all its penalty on your behalf and in your stead. Henceforth, you are the redeemed of the Lord, and enjoy a liberty that comes by no other way but that of the eternal ransom.

Remember this glorious truth, and whenever you feel most assured that you are a child of God, praise the redeeming blood. Whenever your heart beats highest with love for your great Father, bless the *"firstborn among many brethren"* (Rom. 8:29). For your sakes, He came under the law, was circumcised, kept the law in His life, and bowed His head to it in His death. He honored and magnified the law, and made the justice and righteousness of God to be more conspicuous by His life than it would have been by the holiness of all mankind, and God's justice to be more fully vindicated by His death than it would have been if all the world of sinners had been cast into hell. Glory be to our redeeming Lord, by whom we have received the adoption!

PRIVILEGE

Again, we further learn from the passage that we now enjoy the privilege of sonship. According to the context of the passage, the apostle means not only that we are children, but also that we are full-grown sons. *"Because ye are sons"* means that because the time appointed by the Father has come, and you are of age, you are no longer under tutors and governors. As minors, we are under the authority of the schoolmaster, under the regimen of ceremonies, under types, figures, shadows, learning our ABCs by being convinced of sin; but when faith comes, we are no longer under the schoolmaster, but come to a more free condition. Until faith comes, we are under tutors and governors, like mere boys, but after faith comes, we take our rights as sons of God.

The Jewish church of old was under the yoke of the law; its sacrifices were continual and its ceremonies endless; new moons and feasts had to be kept; jubilees had to be observed and pilgrimages made. In fact, the yoke was too heavy for feeble flesh to bear. The law followed the Israelite into every corner, and dealt with him upon every point. It had to do with his clothing, his food, his drink, his bed, his board, and everything about him. It treated him like a boy at school who has a rule for everything.

Now that faith has come, we are full-grown sons; therefore, we are free from the rules that govern the child. We are under law to Christ, even as the full-grown son is still under the discipline of his father's house; but this is a law of love and not of fear, of grace and not of bondage. *"Stand fast therefore in the liberty wherewith Christ hath made us free, and be not entangled again with the yoke of bondage"* (Gal. 5:1). Do not return to the beggarly elements of a merely outward religion, but keep close to the worship of God in spirit and in truth, for this is the liberty of the children of God.

Now, by faith we are no more like servants. The apostle says that *"the heir, as long as he is a child, differeth nothing from a servant, though he be lord of all; but is under tutors and governors until the time appointed of the father"* (Gal. 4:1–2). But, beloved, now you are the sons of God, and you have come to your majority. Now you are free to enjoy the honors and blessings of the Father's house. Rejoice that the free spirit dwells within you and prompts you to holiness; this is a far superior power to the merely external command and the whip of threatening. Now you are no longer in bondage to outward forms, rites, and ceremonies, but the Spirit of God teaches you all things and leads you into the inner meaning and substance of the truth.

INHERITANCE

Now, also, said the apostle, we are heirs: *"Wherefore thou art no more a servant, but a son; and if a son, then an heir of God through Christ"* (Gal. 4:7). No man living has ever realized to the full what this means. Believers are at this moment heirs, but what is the estate? It is God Himself! We are heirs of God—not only of the promises, of the covenant engagements, and of all the blessings that belong to the chosen seed, but heirs of God Himself! *"The LORD is my portion, saith my soul"* (Lam. 3:24). *"This God is our God for ever and ever"* (Ps. 48:14). We are not only heirs to God, to all that He gives to His firstborn, but also heirs of God Himself. David said, *"The LORD is the portion of mine inheritance and of my cup"* (Ps. 16:5). As God said to Abraham, *"Fear not, Abram: I am thy shield, and thy exceeding great reward"* (Gen. 15:1), so He says to every man who is born of the Spirit. These are His own words: *"I will be to them a God, and they shall be to me a people"* (Heb. 8:10).

Why, then, believer, are you poor? All riches are yours. Why, then, are you sorrowful? The ever blessed God is yours. Why do you tremble? Omnipotence waits to help you. Why do you distrust? His immutability will abide with you even to the end, and make His promise steadfast. All things are yours, for Christ is yours, and Christ is God's. Although there are some things that at present you cannot actually grasp in your hand, or even see with your eyes, namely, the things that are laid up for you in heaven, still, by faith, you can enjoy even these, for God has *"raised us up together, and made us sit together in heavenly places in Christ Jesus"* (Eph. 2:6), *"in whom also we have obtained an inheritance"* (Eph. 1:11), so that *"our citizenship is in heaven"* (Phil. 3:20 NKJV). Even now, we enjoy the pledge and guarantee of heaven in the indwelling of the Holy Spirit. Oh, what privileges belong to those who are the sons of God!

OPPOSITION

I would like to make one more point regarding the believer's dignity: we are already tasting one of the inevitable consequences of being the sons of God. What are they? One of them is the opposition of the children of the bondwoman. (See Galatians 4:22–29.) No sooner had the apostle Paul preached the liberty of the saints than immediately there arose certain teachers who said, "This will never do; you must be circumcised. You must come under the law." (See Acts 15:1–31; Galatians 5:11.) Their opposition was to Paul a token that he was of the freewoman, for behold the children of the bondwoman singled him out for their virulent opposition. You will find, dear friend, that if you enjoy fellowship with God, if you live in the spirit of adoption, if you are brought near to the Most High, so as to be a member of the divine family, immediately all those who are under bondage to the law will quarrel with you. Thus said the apostle, *"As then he that was born after the flesh perse- cuted him that was born after the Spirit, even so it is now"* (Gal. 4:29).

The child of Hagar was found by Sarah to be mocking Isaac, the child of promise (Gen. 21:8–9). Ishmael would have been glad to have shown his enmity to the hated heir by blows and personal assault, but there was a superior power to check him, so that he could get no further than "mocking." So it is now.

There have been periods in which the enemies of the Gospel have gone a great deal further than mocking, for they have been able to imprison and burn alive the lovers of the Gospel; but now, thank God, we are under His special protection as to life and limb and liberty, and are as safe as Isaac was in Abraham's house. They can mock us, but they cannot go any further, or else some of us would be publicly tried. But trials of cruel mocking are still to be endured: our words are twisted, our sentiments are misrepresented, and all sorts of horrible things are imputed to us, things that we know not, to all which we would reply with Paul, *"Am I therefore become your enemy, because I tell you the truth?"* (Gal. 4:16). This is the old way of the Hagarenes. The child after the flesh is still doing his best to mock him who is born after the Spirit. Do not be astonished, neither be grieved in the least degree, when this happens to any of you, but let this also establish your confidence and confirm your faith in Christ Jesus, for He told you of old, *"If ye were of the world, the world would love his own: but because ye are not of the world, but I have chosen you out of the world, therefore the world hateth you"* (John 15:19).

THE CONSEQUENT INDWELLING OF THE HOLY SPIRIT

"God hath sent forth the Spirit of his Son into your hearts." Here is a divine act of the Father. The

Holy Spirit proceeds from the Father and the Son, and God has sent Him forth into your hearts. If He had come only knocking at your hearts and asking your permission to enter, He would never have entered, but when Jehovah sent Him, He made His way, without violating your will, yet with irresistible power. Where Jehovah sent Him, there He will abide and never leave.

THE SPIRIT OF CHRIST

Beloved, I have no time to dwell upon the words of the following Scripture, but I want you to turn them over in your thoughts, for they contain a great depth. As surely as God sent His Son into the world to dwell among men, so that His saints beheld His glory, the *"(glory as of the only begotten of the Father,) full of grace and truth"* (John 1:14), so surely has God sent forth the Spirit to enter into men's hearts, to take up His residence there, that in Him also the glory of God may be revealed. Bless and adore the Lord who has sent you such a Visitor as this.

Now, note the style and title under which the Holy Spirit comes to us: He comes as the Spirit of Jesus. The words are *"the Spirit of his Son,"* by which is not meant the character and disposition of Christ—though that is quite true, for God sends these to His people—but the Holy Spirit.

Why, then, is He called the Spirit of His Son, or the Spirit of Jesus? May we not give these reasons? It was by the Holy Spirit that the human nature of Christ was born of the Virgin. By the Spirit our Lord was attested at His baptism, when the Holy Spirit descended upon Him like a dove, and abode upon

Him. In Him the Holy Spirit dwelt without measure, anointing Him for His great work, and by the Spirit He was anointed with the oil of gladness above His fellows.

The Spirit was also with Him, attesting His ministry by signs and wonders. The Holy Spirit is our Lord's great gift to the church; it was after His ascension that He bestowed the gifts of Pentecost, and the Holy Spirit descended upon the church to abide with the people of God forever. The Holy Spirit is the Spirit of Christ, because He is Christ's witness here below, as well; for *"there are three that bear witness in earth, the Spirit, and the water, and the blood"* (1 John 5:8). For these, and many other reasons, He is called *"the Spirit of his Son,"* and it is He who comes to dwell in believers.

I would urge you very solemnly and gratefully to consider the wondrous condescension that is here displayed. God Himself, the Holy Spirit, takes up His residence in believers. I never know which is more wonderful, the incarnation of Christ or the indwelling of the Holy Spirit. Jesus dwelled here for a while in human flesh, untainted by sin, holy, harmless, undefiled, and separate from sinners; but the Holy Spirit dwells continually in the hearts of all believers, though as yet they are imperfect and prone to evil. Year after year, century after century, He still abides in the saints, and will do so until the elect are all in glory. While we adore the incarnate Son, let us adore also the indwelling Spirit whom the Father has sent.

THE SPIRIT'S RESIDENCE

Now notice the place wherein He takes up His residence: *"God hath sent forth the Spirit of his Son into your hearts."* Note that it does not say that God has sent His Spirit into your heads or your brains. The Spirit of God undoubtedly illuminates the intellect and guides the judgment, but this is not the beginning or the main part of His work. He comes chiefly to the affections; He dwells with the heart, *"for with the heart man believeth unto righteousness"* (Rom. 10:10), and *"God hath sent forth the Spirit of his Son into your hearts."*

Now, the heart is the center of our being; therefore, the Holy Spirit occupies this place of strategic advantage. He comes into the central fortress and universal citadel of our nature, and thus takes possession of the whole. The heart is the vital part; we speak of it as the chief residence of life. The Holy Spirit enters it, and as the living God, dwells in the living heart, taking possession of the very core and marrow of our being. It is from the heart and through the heart that life is diffused. The blood is sent even to the extremities of the body by the pulsing of the heart, and when the Spirit of God takes possession of the affections, He operates upon every power, faculty, and member of our entire personhood. Out of the heart are the issues of life; from the affections sanctified by the Holy Spirit, all other faculties and powers receive renewal, illumination, sanctification, strengthening, and ultimate perfection.

THE SPIRIT'S BLESSING

This wonderful blessing is ours *"because* [we] *are sons."* It is fraught with marvelous results. Sonship sealed by the indwelling Spirit brings us peace and joy. It leads to nearness to God and fellowship with Him. It excites trust, love, and vehement desire and creates in us reverence, obedience, and actual likeness to God. All of this occurs, and much more, because the Holy Spirit has come to dwell in us. Oh, matchless mystery! Had it not been revealed, it had never been imagined; now that it is revealed, it would never have been believed, if it had not become a matter of actual experience to those who are in Christ Jesus.

Many who profess to know Christ know nothing of this reality. They listen to us with bewilderment as if we told them an idle tale, for the carnal mind does not know the things that are of God; they are spiritual and can only be spiritually discerned. Those who are not sons, or who only come in as sons under the law of nature, like Ishmael, know nothing of this indwelling Spirit, and are up in arms at us for daring to claim so great a blessing. Yet it is ours, and none can deprive us of it.

THE FILIAL CRY

Now I come to the third portion of our text. This point is deeply interesting, and I think it will be profitable to you if your minds enter into it. Where the Holy Spirit enters, there is a cry: *"God hath sent forth the Spirit of his Son...crying, Abba, Father."*

THE SPIRIT CRIES

Now, notice, it is the Spirit of God who cries—a most remarkable fact. Some are inclined to view the expression as a Hebraism, and read it, He "makes us to cry"; but, beloved, the text does not say this, and we are not at liberty to alter it upon such a pretense. We are always right in keeping to what God says, and here we plainly read of the Spirit in our hearts that He is crying, *"Abba, Father."* The apostle in Romans 8:15 said, *"Ye have received the Spirit of adoption, whereby we cry, Abba, Father,"* but here he describes the Spirit Himself as *"crying, Abba, Father."* We are certain that when he ascribed the cry of *"Abba, Father"* to us, he did not wish to exclude the Spirit's cry, because in the twenty-sixth verse of the famous eighth chapter of Romans, he said,

> *Likewise the Spirit also helpeth our infirmities: for we know not what we should pray for as we ought: but the Spirit itself maketh intercession for us with groanings which cannot be uttered.*

THE SPIRIT GROANS

Thus he represents the Spirit Himself as groaning with unutterable groanings within the child of God, so that when he wrote to the Romans he had on his mind the same thought that he here expressed to the Galatians—that it is the Spirit Himself who cries and groans in us *"Abba, Father."* How is this possible? Is it not ourselves who cry? Yes, assuredly; and yet the Spirit cries also. The expressions are both correct. The Holy Spirit prompts and inspires the cry. He puts the cry into the heart and mouth of the believer. It is His cry because He suggests it, approves of it, and educates us to it. We would never have cried thus, if He had not first taught us the way. As a mother teaches her child to speak, so He puts this cry of "Abba, Father" into our mouths; yes, it is He who forms the desire after our Father God and keeps it there in our hearts. He is the Spirit of adoption, and the author of adoption's special and significant cry.

THE SPIRIT CRIES FOR US

He not only prompts us to cry but also works in us a sense of need that compels us to cry, and a spirit of confidence that emboldens us to claim such relationship to the great God. Nor is this all, for He assists us in some mysterious manner so that we are able to pray correctly. He puts His divine energy into us so that we cry "Abba, Father" in an acceptable manner. There are times when we cannot cry at all, and then He cries in us. There are seasons when doubts and fears abound and suffocate us with their fumes, so that we cannot even raise a cry. Then the indwelling Spirit represents us, speaks for us, and makes intercession for us, crying in our name, and making intercession for us according to the will of God. Thus does the cry "Abba, Father" rise up in our hearts even when we feel as if we could not pray and dare not think of ourselves as God's children. Then we may each say, "I live, yet not I, but the Spirit who dwells in me." (See Galatians 2:20.)

THE SPIRIT CRIES THROUGH US

On the other hand, at times, our soul gives such a sweet assent to the Spirit's cry that it becomes ours also; but then we more than ever own the work of the Spirit and still ascribe to Him the blessed cry, *"Abba, Father."*

It Is the Cry of the Son

I want you now to notice a very sweet fact about this cry, namely, that it is literally the cry of the Son. God has sent the Spirit of His Son into our hearts, and that Spirit cries in us exactly according to the cry of the Son. If you turn to Mark 14:36, you will find there what you will not discover in any other gospel (for Mark is always the man for the striking points and the memorable words). He records that our Lord prayed in the garden, *"Abba, Father, all things are possible unto thee; take away this cup from me: nevertheless not what I will, but what thou wilt."* Therefore, this cry in us copies the cry of our Lord to the letter—*"Abba, Father."*

The Cry Is in His Native Tongue

I daresay that you have heard these words *"Abba, Father"* explained at considerable length at other times, and if so, you know that the first word is Syrian or Aramaic; or, roughly speaking, *Abba* is the Hebrew word for "father." The second word is in Greek and is the Gentile word *pates,* or *pater,* which also signifies father. It is said that these two words are used to remind us that Jews and Gentiles are one before God. They do remind us of this, but this cannot have been the principal reason for their use. Do you think that, when our Lord was in His agony in the garden, He said *"Abba, Father"* because Jews and Gentiles are one? Why would He have thought of that doctrine, and why would He need to mention it in prayer to His Father? Some other reason must have suggested it to Him.

It seems to me that our Lord said *"Abba"* because it was His native tongue. When a Frenchman prays, if he has learned English, he may ordinarily pray in English, but if he ever falls into an agony, he will pray in French, as surely as he prays at all. Our Welsh brethren tell us that there is no language like Welsh. I suppose that is true for them. Now, they will speak English when they talk about their ordinary business, and they can pray in English when everything goes comfortably with them, but I am sure that if a Welshman is in a great fervency of prayer, he flies to his Welsh tongue to find full expression. Our Lord in His agony used His native language, and as born of the seed of Abraham He cried in His own tongue, *"Abba."* Even thus, my brethren, we are prompted by the Spirit of adoption to use our own language, the language of the heart, and to speak to the Lord freely in our own tongue.

IT IS THE CRY OF A CHILD

Besides, to my mind, the word *Abba* is of all words in all languages the most natural word for father. I must try to pronounce it so that you see the natural childishness of it, "Ab...ba," "Ab...ba." Is it not just what your children say, "Ab...ab...ba...ba," as soon as they try to talk? It is the sort of word that any child would say, whether Hebrew or Greek or French or English. Therefore, *Abba* is a word worthy of introduction into all languages. It is truly a child's word, and our Master felt, I have no doubt, in His agony, a love for a child's words.

Dr. Guthrie, when he was dying, said, "Sing a hymn," but he added, "Sing me one of the bairns' hymns." When a man comes to die, he wants to be a child again, and longs for bairns' hymns and bairns' words. Our blessed Master in His agony used the bairns' word, *"Abba,"* and it is equally becoming in the mouth of each one of us.

I think this sweet word *"Abba"* was chosen to show us that we are to be very natural with God, and not stilted and formal. We are to be very affectionate, come close to Him, and not merely say "Pater," which is a cold Greek word, but "Abba," which is a warm, natural, loving word, fit for one who is a little child with God, who boldly lies on His bosom and looks up into His face and talks with holy boldness. "Abba" is not a word, somehow, but a babe's lisping. Oh, how near we are to God when we can use such speech! How dear He is to us and dear we are to Him when we may thus address Him, saying, like the great Son Himself, *"Abba, Father."*

The Cry Is Childlike in Nature

This leads me to observe that this cry in our hearts is exceedingly near and familiar. I have shown you that the sound of it is childlike, but the tone and manner of the utterance are equally so. Note that it is a cry. If we obtain audience with a king, we do not cry. We speak then in measured tones and set phrases, but the Spirit of God breaks down our measured tones and takes away the formality that some hold in great admiration, and He leads us to cry, which is the very reverse of formality and stiffness. When we cry, we cry, "Abba."

Even our very cries are full of the Spirit of adoption. A cry is a sound that we are not anxious that every passerby should hear, yet what child minds his father hearing him cry? So when our heart is broken and subdued, we do not feel as if we could speak fine language at all, but the Spirit in us sends forth cries and groans, and of these we are not ashamed, nor are we afraid to cry before God. I know some of you think that God will not hear your prayers, because you cannot pray grandly like such-and-such a minister. Oh, but the Spirit of His Son cries, and you cannot do better than cry, too. Be satisfied to offer to God broken language, words salted with your griefs, wetted with your tears. Go to Him with holy familiarity, and do not be afraid to cry in His presence, *"Abba, Father."*

THE CRY IS EARNEST

But then how earnest it is, for a cry is an intense thing. The word implies fervency. A cry is not a flippant utterance, or a mere thing of the lips; it comes up from the soul. Has not the Lord taught us to cry to Him in prayer with fervent importunity that will not take a denial? Has He not brought us so near to Him that sometimes we say, *"I will not let thee go, except thou bless me"*? (Gen. 32:26.) Has He not taught us so to pray that His disciples might almost say of us as they did of one of old, *"Send her away; for she crieth after us"* (Matt. 15:23)? We do cry after Him; our hearts and our flesh cry out for God, for the living God, and this is the cry, "Abba, Father, I must know You. I must taste Your love. I must dwell under Your wing. I must behold Your face. I must feel Your great fatherly heart overflowing and filling my heart with peace." We cry, *"Abba, Father."*

THE CRY COMES FROM THE HEART

In closing, note that most of this crying is kept within the heart and does not come out of the lips. Like Moses, we cry when we do not say a word. God has sent forth the Spirit of His Son into our hearts, *"whereby we cry, Abba, Father."* You know what I mean: it is not alone in your little room, by the old armchair, that you cry to God, but you call Him *"Abba, Father"* as you go about the streets or work in the shop. The Spirit of His Son is crying *"Abba, Father"* when you are in the crowd or at your table among the family. I see it is alleged as a very grave charge against me that I speak as if I were familiar with God. If it is so, I boldly say that I speak only as I feel. Blessed be my heavenly Father's name. I know I am His child, and with whom should a child be familiar but with his father? Strangers to the living God, be it known to you that if this is vile, I purpose to be viler still, as He will help me to walk more closely with Him. We feel a deep reverence for our Father in heaven, which bows us to the very dust, but for all that, we can say, *"Truly our fellowship is with the Father, and with his Son Jesus Christ"* (1 John 1:3).

No stranger can understand the nearness of the believer's soul to God in Christ Jesus. Because the world cannot understand it, it finds it convenient to sneer, but what of that? Abraham's tenderness to Isaac made Ishmael jealous and caused him to laugh, but Isaac had no cause to be ashamed of being ridiculed, since the mocker could not rob him of the covenant blessing.

Yes, beloved, the Spirit of God makes you cry, *"Abba, Father,"* but the cry is mainly within your heart, and there it is so commonly uttered that it becomes the habit of your soul to be crying to your heavenly Father. The text does not say that the Spirit *had cried,* but rather, it uses the word *"crying."* It is a present participle, indicating that He cries every day, *"Abba, Father."*

LIVE IN THE FATHER'S LOVE

Friends, live in the spirit of sonship. Wake up in the morning, and let your first thought be, "My Father, my Father, be with me this day." Go out into business, and when things perplex you, let this be your resort: "My Father, help me in this hour of need." When you go to your home, and there meet with domestic anxieties, let your cry still be, "Help me, my Father." When alone, you are not alone, because the Father is with you; in the midst of the crowd, you are not in danger, because the Father Himself loves you. What a blessed word this is: the Father Himself loves you!

Go and live as His children. Take heed that you reverence Him, for if He is your Father, where is your respect and awe for Him? Go and obey Him, for this is right. *"Be imitators of God as dear children"* (Eph. 5:1 NKJV). Honor Him wherever you are, by adorning His doctrine in all things. Go and live upon Him, for you will soon live with Him. Go and rejoice in Him. Go and cast all your cares upon Him. Go, henceforth, and whatever men may see in you may they be compelled to admit that you are the children of the Highest. *"Blessed are the peacemakers, for they shall be called sons of God"* (Matt. 5:9 NKJV). May you be such henceforth and evermore. Amen and amen.

Chapter 7

Grieving the Holy Spirit

And grieve not the holy Spirit of God, whereby ye
are sealed unto the day of redemption.
—Ephesians 4:30

There is something very touching in this admonition, *"Grieve not the holy Spirit of God."* It does not say, "Do not make Him angry." A more delicate and tender term is used—*"Grieve not."* There are some men of so hard a character that to make another person angry does not give them much pain; indeed, there are many of us who are scarcely moved by the information that someone is angry with us. But where is the heart so hard that it is not moved when it knows that it has caused others grief?

Grief is a sweet combination of anger and of love. It is anger, but all the bitterness is taken from it. Love sweetens the anger and turns the edge of it not against the person, but against the offense. We all know how we use the two terms in contradistinction to each other. When I commit any offense, some friend who has but little patience suddenly loses his temper and is angry with me. The same offense is observed by a loving father, and he is grieved. There is anger in his heart, but he is angry and he sins not (Eph. 4:26). He is angry against my sin, yet there is love to neutralize and modify the anger toward me. Instead of wishing me ill as the punishment for my sin, he looks on my sin itself as being the problem. He grieves to think that I am already injured, from the fact that I have sinned. I say grief is a heavenly compound, more precious than all the ointment of the merchants. There may be the bitterness of myrrh, but there is all the sweetness of frankincense in this sweet term "to grieve."

I am certain, my readers, I do not flatter you when I declare that I am sure that most of you would grieve if you thought you were hurting anyone else. Perhaps you would not care much if you had made anyone angry without a cause; but to grieve him, even though it was done without a cause and without intention, would nevertheless cause you distress of heart. You would not rest until this grief had subsided, until you had made some explanation or apology, or had done your best to alleviate the pain and take away the grief.

When we see anger in another, we at once begin to feel hostility. Anger begets anger, but grief begets pity. Pity is similar to love, and we love those whom we have caused to grieve. Now, is this not a very sweet expression: *"Grieve not the holy Spirit"*? Of course, the language is be to understood as speaking after the manner of men. The Holy Spirit of God knows no passion or suffering; nevertheless, His emotion is described here in human language as being that of grief. And is it not a tender and touching thing that the Holy Spirit should direct His servant Paul to have said to us, *"Grieve not the holy Spirit,"* that is, do not excite His loving anger, do not vex

Him, and do not cause Him to mourn? He is a dove; do not cause Him to mourn because you have treated Him harshly and ungratefully.

Now, the purpose of my sermon will be to exhort you not to grieve the Spirit. I will divide it into three sections: first, I will focus on the love of the Spirit; second, on the seal of the Spirit; third, on the grieving of the Spirit.

THE LOVE OF THE SPIRIT

The few words I have to say about the love of the Spirit will all be pressing us forward to my great goal: to stir you up not to grieve the Spirit. When we are persuaded that someone loves us, we find at once a very potent reason why we should not grieve him.

How will I describe the love of the Spirit? Surely it needs a songster to sing it, for love is to be spoken of only in words of song. The love of the Spirit! Let me tell you of His early love for us. He loved us without beginning. In the eternal covenant of grace, He was one of the high contracting parties in the divine contract whereby we are saved.

All that can be said of the love of the Father and of the love of the Son may be said of the love of the Spirit: it is eternal, infinite, sovereign, and everlasting. It is a love that cannot be dissolved, decreased, or removed from those who are the objects of it.

HE SEEKS

Permit me, however, to refer you to His acts, rather than His attributes. Let me tell you of the love of the Spirit for you and me. Oh, how early was that love that He manifested toward us, even in our childhood! My friends, we can well remember how the Spirit was inclined to reach us. We went astray from the womb, speaking lies, but how early did the Spirit of God stir up our consciences and solemnly correct us because of our youthful sins!

How frequently since then has the Spirit wooed us! How often under the ministry has He compelled our hearts to melt and tears to run down our cheeks! He has sweetly whispered in our ears, "My child, give Me your heart. Go to your room, shut the door behind you, confess your sins, and seek the Savior's love and blood."

Oh—let us blush to tell it—how often have we done malice to Him! When we were unregenerate, how we were inclined to resist Him! We quenched the Spirit. He sought us, but we fought Him. But blessed be His dear name, and let Him have everlasting songs, for He would not let us go! We would not be saved, but He would save us. We sought to thrust ourselves into the fire, but He sought to pluck us from the burning. We would dash ourselves from the precipice, but He wrestled with us and held us fast. He would not let us destroy our souls.

Oh, how we mistreated Him! How we discounted His counsel! How we scorned and scoffed at Him! How we despised the laws that would lead us to Christ! How we violated that holy cord that was gently drawing us to Jesus and His Cross! I am sure, my friends, as you remember the persevering struggles of the Spirit with you, you must be stirred up to love Him.

How often He restrained you from sin when you were about to plunge headlong into a course of vice!

How often did He constrain you to good when you would have neglected it! You, perhaps, would not have been in the right place at all, and the Lord would not have met you, if it had not been for that sweet Spirit, who would not let you become a blasphemer, who would not permit you to forsake the house of God, and would not allow you to become a regular attendant at immoral establishments.

Instead, He checked you and held you in, as it were, with bit and bridle. Though you were like a young bull, unaccustomed to the yoke, He would not let you have your way. Though you struggled against Him, He would not throw the reins on your neck. Instead, He said, "I will have him. I will have him against his will. I will change his heart. I will not let him go until I have made him a trophy of My mighty power to save."

Then think of the love of the Spirit after that:

> Dost mind the time, the spot of land,
> Where Jesus did thee meet?
> Where He first took thee by the hand,
> Thy bridegroom's love—how sweet!

HE GUIDES

Ah, then, in that blest hour, to memory dear, was it not the Holy Spirit who guided you to Jesus? Do you remember the love of the Spirit, when, after having quickened you, He took you aside, and showed you Jesus on the tree? Who was it that opened your blind eyes to see a dying Savior? Who was it that opened your deaf ears to hear the voice of pardoning love? Who opened your clasped and palsied hands to receive the tokens of a Savior's grace?

Who was it that broke your hard heart and made a way for the Savior to enter and dwell therein? Oh, it was that precious Spirit, that same Spirit, to whom you had done so much malice, whom in the days of your flesh you had resisted!

What a mercy it was that He did not say, "I will swear in My wrath that they will not enter into My rest, for they have vexed Me. I will take My everlasting flight from them." And since that time, my beloved, how sweetly has the Spirit proved His love for you and me. How much have we owed to His instruction—not only in His first endeavors, and then His divine quickenings, but also in all His actions that have followed!

We have been dull students with the Word before us. It is so plain and simple that he who reads it may understand. Yet how small a portion of His Word has our memory retained; how little progress have we made in the school of God's grace! We are but learners yet, unstable, weak, and apt to slide, but what a blessed Instructor we have! Has He not led us into many truths and taken the things of Christ and applied them to us? Oh, when I think how stupid I have been, I wonder that He has not given up on me. When I think what a dolt I have been, when He would have taught me the things of the kingdom of God, I marvel that He should have had such patience with me.

It is amazing that Jesus would become a baby. Is it not equally amazing that the Spirit of the living God would become a teacher of babes? It is a marvel that Jesus would lie in a manger; is it not an equal marvel that the Holy Spirit would become an assistant teacher in the sacred school, to teach fools and make them wise? It was condescension that brought the Savior to the Cross, but is it not equal condescension that brings the mighty Spirit of grace down to dwell among stubborn, unruly, perverse men, to teach them the mystery of the kingdom and make them know the wonders of a Savior's love?

HE GIVES COMFORT

Furthermore, do not forget how much we owe to the Spirit's consolation. How much has He manifested His love for you in cherishing you in all your sicknesses, assisting you in all your work, and comforting you in all your troubles! He has been a blessed Comforter to me, I can testify. When every other comfort fails, when the promise itself seems empty, when the ministry is void of power, it is then that the Holy Spirit has proved a rich comfort to my soul and filled my poor heart with peace and joy in believing.

How many times would your heart have broken if the Spirit had not bound it up? How often has He who is your Teacher also become your Physician? He has closed the wounds of your poor bleeding spirit and bound up those wounds with the healing balm of the promise. Thus He has stopped the bleeding and has given you back your spiritual health once more. It does seem miraculous that the Holy Spirit should become a Comforter, for comforting is, to many minds, an inferior work in the church, though really it is not so. To teach, to preach, to command with authority, how many are willing to do these things because they are honorable work? But to sit down and bear with the infirmities of a weak person, to deal with the deceit of unbelievers, to find a way of peace for a soul in the midst of seas of trouble—these things require being compassionate as God is compassionate.

How wonderful that the Holy Spirit should stoop from heaven to become a comforter of disconsolate spirits. What! Must He Himself bring the medicine? Must He wait upon His sick child and stand by his bed? Must He make his bed for him in his afflictions? Must He carry him in his infirmity? Must He breathe continually into him His very breath? Does the Holy Spirit become a waiting servant of the church? Does He become a lamp to illuminate? Does He become a staff on which we may lean? This, I say, should move us to love the Holy Spirit, for we have in all this abundant proofs of His love for us.

HE HELPS OUR WEAKNESSES

Do not stop here, beloved, for there are larger fields beyond, now that we are speaking of the love of the Spirit. Remember how much He loves us when He helps our infirmities (Rom. 8:26). He not only helps our infirmities, but also teaches us how to pray when we do not know what to pray for. When *"we ourselves groan within ourselves"* (v. 23), then the Spirit Himself intercedes for us *"with groanings which cannot be uttered"* (v. 26)—groans as we should groan, but more audibly, so that our prayers, which otherwise would have been silent, reach the ears of Christ and are then presented before the Father's face.

To help our infirmities is a mighty example of love. When God overcomes infirmity altogether, or removes it, there is something very noble, grand, and sublime in the deed. When He permits the infirmity to remain and yet works with the infirmity, this is tender compassion indeed. When the Savior heals the lame man, you see His Godhead, but when He walks with the lame man, limping though his gait may be; when He sits with the beggar; when He talks with the publican; when He carries the baby close to His heart, then this helping of infirmities is a manifestation of love almost unequalled.

Except for Christ's bearing our infirmities and *"our sins in his own body on the tree"* (1 Pet. 2:24), I know of no greater or more tender instance of divine love than when it is written, *"Likewise the Spirit also helpeth our infirmities"* (Rom. 8:26). Oh, how much you owe to the Spirit when you have been on your knees in prayer! You know, my brethren, what it is to be dull and lifeless there; to groan for a word, and yet you cannot find it; to wish for a word, and yet the very wish is weak; to long to have desires, and yet all the desire you have is a desire that you may be able to desire.

Oh, have you not sometimes, when your desires have been kindled, longed to grasp hold of the promises by the hand of faith? "Oh," you have said, "if I could but plead the promises, all my needs would be removed, and all my sorrows would be lessened." Sadly, the promise was beyond your reach. If you touched it with the tip of your finger, you could not grasp it as you desired, you could not plead it, and therefore you came away without the blessing.

But when the Spirit has helped our infirmities, how we have prayed! Why, there have been times when you and I have so grasped the knocker of the gate of mercy, and have let it fall with such tremendous force, that it seemed as if the very gate itself shook and tottered. There have been seasons when we have laid hold upon the angel, have overcome heaven by prayer, and have declared we would not let Jehovah Himself go unless He would bless us. (See Genesis 32:24–26.) We have, and we say it without blasphemy, moved the arm that moves the world. We have brought down upon us the eyes that look upon the universe. All this we have done, not by our own strength, but by the might and by the power of the Spirit. Seeing He has so sweetly enabled us, though we have so often forgotten to thank Him; seeing that He has so graciously assisted us, though we have often taken all the glory to ourselves instead of crediting it to Him; must we not admire His love, and must it not be a fearful sin indeed to grieve the Holy Spirit by whom we are sealed?

HE LIVES WITHIN

Another token of the Spirit's love remains, namely, His indwelling in the saints. We sing in one of our hymns, "Dost Thou not dwell in all the saints?" We ask a question that can have only one answer. He *does* dwell in the hearts of all God's redeemed and blood-washed people. And what a condescension this is, my friend, that He whom the heaven of heavens cannot contain dwells in your heart. Although that heart is often covered with rags or agitated with anxious cares and thoughts, although it is too often defiled with sin, He dwells there. The Holy Spirit has made the little narrow heart of man His palace. Though it is but a cottage, a very hovel, and

all unholy and unclean, yet the Holy Spirit conde-
scends to make the hearts of His people His continual home. Oh, my friends, when I think how often
you and I have let the Devil in, I wonder why the
Spirit has not withdrawn from us.

The final perseverance of the saints is one of the
greatest miracles on record; in fact, it is the sum to-
tal of miracles. The perseverance of a saint for a single day is a multitude of miracles of mercy. When
you consider that the Spirit is of purer eyes than to
behold iniquity, yet He dwells in the heart where sin
often intrudes, a heart out of which come blasphe-
mies, murders, and all manner of evil thoughts and
sexual desires, what if sometimes He is grieved and
retires and leaves us to ourselves for a season? It is a
marvel that He is there at all, for He must be daily
grieved with these evil guests, these false traitors,
these base intruders who thrust themselves into that
little temple that He has honored with His presence,
the temple of the heart of man.

I am afraid, dear friends, that we are too much
in the habit of talking about the love of Jesus, without thinking about the love of the Holy Spirit. Now, I
would not wish to exalt one person of the Trinity
above another, but I do feel that because Jesus
Christ was a man, bone of our bone, and flesh of our
flesh (see Genesis 2:23), and therefore there was
something tangible in Him that could be seen with
the eyes and handled with the hands, therefore we
more readily think of Him and fix our love on Him
than we do upon the Spirit.

But why should this be? Let us love Jesus with
all our hearts, and let us love the Holy Spirit, too.
Let us have songs for Him, gratitude for Him. Just

as we do not forget Christ's Cross, let us not forget the Spirit's operations. We do not forget what Jesus has done for us; therefore, let us always remember what the Spirit does in us. Why do you talk of the love, grace, tenderness, and faithfulness of Christ, when you do not say the same things about the Spirit? Was ever love like His, that He should visit us? Was ever mercy like His, that He should bear with our bad manners, though we repeatedly do the same things? Was ever faithfulness like His, that multitudes of sins cannot drive Him away? Was ever power like His, which overcomes all our iniquities, and yet leads us safely on, though hosts of foes within and without would rob us of our Christian life?

> Oh, the love of the Spirit I sing
> By whom is redemption applied.

And unto His name be glory forever and ever.

THE SEAL OF THE SPIRIT

This brings me to the second point. Here we have another reason why we should not grieve the Spirit: it is by the Holy Spirit that we are sealed. By the Spirit, we *are sealed unto the day of redemption.* I will be very brief here. The Spirit Himself is expressed as the seal, even as He Himself is directly said to be the pledge of our inheritance. The sealing, I think, has a threefold meaning.

A SEAL OF CONFIRMATION

It is a sealing of attestation or confirmation. I want to know whether I am truly a child of God. The

Spirit Himself also bears witness with my spirit that I am born of God (Rom. 8:16). I have the writings, the title deed of the inheritance that is to come. I want to know whether those are valid, whether they are true, or whether they are mere counterfeits written by that old scribe of hell, Master Presumption and Carnal Security.

How am I to know? I look for the seal. After we have believed on the Son of God, the Father seals us as His children, by the gift of the Holy Spirit. *"Now he which...hath anointed us, is God; who hath also sealed us, and given the earnest of the Spirit in our hearts"* (2 Cor. 1:21–22). No faith is genuine that does not bear the seal of the Spirit. No love, no hope, can ever save us, unless it is sealed with the Spirit of God, for whatever does not have His seal upon it is false. Faith that is unsealed may be a poison or a presumption, but faith that is sealed by the Spirit is true, real, genuine faith.

Never be content, my dear readers, unless you are sealed, unless you are assured by the inward witness and testimony of the Holy Spirit that you have been *"begotten...again unto a lively hope by the resurrection of Jesus Christ from the dead"* (1 Pet. 1:3). It is possible for a man to know infallibly that he is secure of heaven. He may not only hope so, but also know beyond a doubt, and he may know it by being able with the eye of faith to see the seal, the broad stamp of the Holy Spirit, set upon his own character and experience. It is a seal of attestation.

A SEAL OF APPROPRIATION

In the next place, it is a sealing of appropriation. When men put their mark upon an article, it is to show that it is their own. The farmer marks his tools so that they will not be stolen. They are his. The shepherd brands his sheep so that they may be recognized as belonging to his flock. The king himself puts his broad arrow upon everything that is his property. So the Holy Spirit puts the broad arm of God upon the hearts of all His people. He seals us. You will *"be mine, saith the LORD of hosts, in that day when I make up my jewels"* (Mal. 3:17).

And then the Spirit puts God's seal upon us to signify that we are God's reserved inheritance, His special people, the portion in which His soul delights. But, again, by sealing is meant preservation. Men seal up what they wish to have preserved, and when a document is sealed, it becomes valid henceforth. Now, it is by the Spirit of God that the Christian is sealed, that he is kept, preserved, *"sealed unto the day of redemption,"* sealed until Christ comes fully to redeem the bodies of His saints by raising them from the dead, and fully to redeem the world by purging it from sin and making it a kingdom unto Himself in righteousness.

If we maintain our position in Christ, we will be saved. The chosen seed cannot be lost; they must be brought home at last, but how? By the sealing of the Spirit. Apart from that they perish; they are undone. When the last general fire blazes out, everything that does not have the seal of the Spirit on it will be burned up. But the men upon whose forehead is the seal will be preserved. They will be safe "amid the wreck of matter and the crash of worlds." Their spirits, mounting above the flames, will dwell with Christ eternally, and with that same seal on their forehead, they will sing the everlasting song of gratitude and praise upon Mount Zion. This is the second reason why we should love the Spirit and why we should not grieve Him.

THE GRIEVING OF THE SPIRIT

I come now to the third part of my message, namely, the grieving of the Spirit. How can we grieve Him, what will be the sad result of grieving Him, and if we have grieved Him, how can we bring Him back again?

THROUGH INWARD AND OUTWARD ACTS OF SIN

How can we grieve the Spirit? I am now, mark you, speaking of those who love the Lord Jesus Christ. The Spirit of God is in your hearts, and it is easy indeed to grieve Him. Sin is as easy as it is wicked. You may grieve Him by impure thoughts. He cannot bear sin. If you indulge in lewd expressions, or even if you allow your imagination to dwell on any impure act, if your heart is covetous, if you set your heart upon anything that is evil, the Spirit of God will be grieved. I hear Him speaking, "I love this man. I want to have his heart, and yet he is entertaining these filthy lusts. His thoughts, instead of running after Me, after Christ, and after the Father are running after the temptations that are in the world through lust." And then His Spirit is grieved. He sorrows in His soul because He knows what sorrow these things must bring to our souls.

We grieve Him still more if we indulge in outward acts of sin. Then sometimes He is so grieved that He takes His flight for a season, for the Dove will not dwell in our hearts if we take loathsome carrion there. The Holy Spirit, the Dove, is a pure being, and we must not strew the place that the Dove frequents with filth and mire. If we do, He will fly elsewhere.

If we commit sin, if we openly bring disgrace upon our religion, if we tempt others to go into iniquity by our evil examples, it is not long before the Holy Spirit will begin to grieve. Again, if we neglect prayer, if our prayer closet is cobwebbed, if we forget to read the Scriptures, if the pages of our Bible are almost stuck together by neglect, if we never seek to do any good in the world, if we live merely for ourselves and not for Christ, then the Holy Spirit will be grieved, for thus He has said,

They have forsaken me the fountain of living waters, and hewed them out cisterns, broken cisterns, that can hold no water. (Jer. 2:13)

I think I now see the Spirit of God grieving when you sit down to read a novel, and there is your Bible unread. Perhaps you take down some travel book, and you forget that you have got a more precious travel book in the Acts of the Apostles and in the story of your blessed Lord and Master. You have no time for prayer, but the Spirit sees you very active about worldly things, having many hours to spare for relaxation and amusement. And then He is grieved because He sees that you love worldly things better than you love Him. His spirit is grieved within Him. Take care that He does not go away from you, for it will be a pitiful thing for you if He leaves you to yourself.

THROUGH INGRATITUDE

Again, ingratitude tends to grieve Him. Nothing cuts a man to the heart more than after having done his utmost to help another, that person turns around and repays him with ingratitude or insult. If we do not want to be thanked, at least we want to know that there is thankfulness in the heart on which we have conferred a blessing. And when the Holy Spirit looks into our soul and sees little love for Christ and no gratitude to Him for all He has done for us, then He is grieved.

THROUGH UNBELIEF

Again, the Holy Spirit is exceedingly grieved by our unbelief. When we distrust the promise He has given and applied, when we doubt the power or the affection of our blessed Lord, then the Spirit says within Himself, "They doubt My fidelity; they distrust My power. They say Jesus is not able to save to the uttermost." (See Hebrews 7:25.) Thus again is the Spirit grieved.

Oh, I wish the Spirit had an advocate here who could express these thoughts in better terms than I can. I have a theme that overmasters me. I seem to grieve for Him, but I cannot make you grieve or express the grief I feel. In my own soul I keep saying, "Oh, this is just what you have done; you have grieved Him." Let me make a full and frank confession before you all. I know that too often, I, as well as you, have grieved the Holy Spirit. Much within us has made that sacred Dove to mourn, and my marvel is that He has not taken His flight from us and left us utterly to ourselves.

WHAT HAPPENS WHEN THE SPIRIT IS GRIEVED?

Now suppose the Holy Spirit is grieved. What is the effect produced upon us? When the Spirit is grieved, first, He bears with us. He is grieved again and again, and again and again, and still He bears with it all. But at last, His grief becomes so excessive that He says, "I will suspend My operations; I will depart. I will leave life behind Me, but My own actual presence I will take away."

When the Spirit of God goes away from us and suspends all His operations, what a miserable state we are in. He suspends His instructions; we read the Word, but we cannot understand it. We go to our commentaries, but they cannot tell us the meaning. We fall on our knees and ask to be taught, but we get no answer; we learn nothing. He suspends His comfort. We used to dance, like David before the ark. (See 2 Samuel 6:13–16.) Now we sit like Job among the ashes and scrape our boils with a potsherd. (See Job 2:7–8.)

There was a time when His candle shone round about us, but now He is gone; He has left us in the blackness of darkness. Now, He takes from us all spiritual power. Once we could *do all things* (Phil. 4:13); now we can do nothing. We could slay the Philistines, and lay them heaps upon heaps, but now Delilah can deceive us, and our eyes are put out and we are made to grind in the mill. (See Judges 15:14–17; 16:4–21.)

We preach, but there is no pleasure in preaching, and no good results come from it. We distribute tracts and attend Sunday school, but we might almost as well be at home. We go through the motions

of being a Christian, but there is no love. There is
the intention to do good, or perhaps not even that,
but alas, there is no power to accomplish the intention. The Lord has withdrawn Himself, His light, His
joy, His comfort, His spiritual power; all are gone.
And then all our graces flag.

Our graces are much like the flower called the
hydrangea; when it has plenty of water, it blooms,
but as soon as moisture fails, the leaves drop down at
once. And so when the Spirit goes away, faith shuts
up its flowers; no perfume is released. Then the fruit
of our love begins to rot and drops from the tree;
then the sweet buds of our hope become frostbitten,
and they die. Oh, what a sad thing it is to lose the
Spirit. Have you never, my beloved, been on your
knees and been conscious that the Spirit of God was
not with you? What awful work it has been to groan,
to cry, to sigh, and yet go away again. No light shines
on the promises, not so much as a ray of light
through the chink of the dungeon. All forsaken, forgotten, and forlorn, you are almost driven to despair.
You sing with Cowper,

> What peaceful hours I once enjoyed,
> How sweet their memory still!
> But they have left an aching void,
> The world can never fill.
> Return, Thou sacred Dove, return,
> Sweet Messenger of rest,
> I hate the sins that made Thee mourn,
> And drove Thee from my breast.
>
> The dearest idol I have known,
> Whate'er that idol be,
> Help me to tear it from its throne,
> And worship only Thee.

It is sad enough to have the Spirit withdraw from us, but I am about to say something with the utmost love, which, perhaps, may sound severe; nevertheless, I must say it. The churches of the present day are very much in the position of those who have grieved the Spirit of God, for the Spirit deals with churches just as it does with individuals.

In recent years, how little has God worked in the midst of His churches. Throughout England, at least some four or five years ago, an almost universal lethargy had fallen upon the visible body of Christ. There was a little action, but it was spasmodic; there was no real vitality. Oh, how few sinners were brought to Christ. How empty had our places of worship become. Our prayer meetings were dwindling away to nothing, and our church meetings were mere matters of farce. You know very well that this is the case with many London churches to this day, and there are some who do not mourn about it. They go to their accustomed place of worship, the minister prays, the people either sleep with their eyes or else with their hearts, they go out, and there is never a soul saved. The pool of baptism is seldom stirred, yet the saddest part of all is this: the churches are willing to have it so. They are not earnest to have a revival of religion.

We have been doing something; the church at large has been doing something. I will not just now put my finger upon what the sin is, but there has been something done that has driven the Spirit of God from us. He is grieved, and He is gone.

But He is present with us here, thank His name. He is still visible in our midst. He has not left us. Though we have been as unworthy as others, yet He has given us a long outpouring of His presence. These last five years or more, we have had a revival that is not to be exceeded by any revival upon the face of the earth. Without cries or shoutings, without fallings down or swooning, steadily God adds to this church numbers upon numbers. Your minister's heart is ready to break with joy when he thinks how manifestly the Spirit of God is with us, but we must not be content with this. We want to see the Spirit poured out on all churches.

Look at the great gatherings that there were in St. Paul's, Westminster Abbey, Exeter Hall, and other places. How was it that no good was done, or so very little? I have watched with anxious eye, and I have never from the time of those gatherings heard but of one conversion—and that was in St. James' Hall—from all these services. It seems strange. The blessing may have come in larger measure than we know, but not in so large a measure as we might have expected, if the Spirit of God had been present with all the ministers. Oh, would that we may live to see greater things than we have ever seen yet. Go home to your houses and humble yourselves before God, members of Christ's church. Cry aloud that He will visit His church, that He would open the windows of heaven and pour out His grace upon His thirsty hill of Zion, that nations may be born in a day, that sinners may be saved by the thousands, and that Zion may travail and may bring forth children.

Oh, there are signs and tokens of a coming revival. We have heard recently of a good work among the Ragged School* boys at St. Giles's, and our souls

---

* Schools started in the late eighteenth century in England to provide free education and other opportunities for poor children.

have been glad on account of that. The news from Ireland comes to us like good tidings, not from a far country, but from a sister province of the kingdom. Let us cry aloud to the Holy Spirit, who is certainly grieved with His church, and let us purge our churches of everything that is contrary to His Word and to sound doctrine. Then the Spirit will return, and His power will be manifest.

In conclusion, there may be some of you who have lost the visible presence of Christ with you—who have, in fact, so grieved the Spirit that He has gone. It is a mercy for you to know that the Spirit of God never leaves His people finally; He leaves them for chastisement, but not for damnation. He sometimes leaves them so that they may benefit from knowing their own weaknesses, but He will not leave them finally to perish.

Are you in a state of backsliding, falling away, and coldness? Listen to me for a moment, and God bless these words. Friend, do not remain for a moment in a condition so perilous. Do not rest easy for a single second in the absence of the Holy Spirit. I beseech you to use every means by which the Spirit may be brought back to you.

Once more, let me tell you distinctly what the means are. Search out the sin that has grieved the Spirit, give it up, and slay that sin upon the spot. Repent with tears and sighs. Continue in prayer, and never rest satisfied until the Holy Spirit comes back to you. Faithfully attend an earnest ministry. Spend much time with sincere saints. But above all, be much in prayer to God, and let your daily cry be, "Return, return, Holy Spirit, return, and dwell in my soul."

Oh, I beseech you not to be content until that prayer is heard, for you have become weak as water, and faint and empty, while the Spirit has been away from you. It may be that there are some reading this message with whom the Spirit has been striving during the past week. Yield to Him; do not resist Him. Do not grieve Him, but yield to Him.

Is the Holy Spirit saying to you now, "Turn to Christ?" Listen to Him. Obey Him, and He will direct you. I beg you, do not despise Him. Have you resisted Him many times? Then take care that you do not resist Him again, for there may come a last time when the Spirit may say, "I will go unto My rest; I will not return to him. The ground is accursed; it will be given up to barrenness."

Hear the word of the Gospel, for the Spirit speaks earnestly to you now in this short sentence: *"Repent ye therefore, and be converted, that your sins may be blotted out, when the times of refreshing shall come from the presence of the Lord"* (Acts 3:19). And hear this solemn sentence: *"He that believeth and is baptized shall be saved; but he that believeth not shall be damned"* (Mark 16:16). May the Lord grant that we may not grieve the Holy Spirit.

Chapter 8

The Holy Spirit and the One Church

These be they who separate themselves, sensual,
having not the Spirit.
—Jude 1:19

When a farmer comes to thrash his wheat and prepare it for market, he desires two things: that there will be plenty of the right type of grain, and that he will have a pure grain to sell. He does not look upon the quantity alone, for of what worth is the chaff to the wheat? He would rather have a smaller amount of a good quality product than a great heap containing a vast quantity of chaff.

On the other hand, he would not so winnow his wheat as to drive away any of the good grain, and thus make the quantity less than it needs to be. He wants to have as much as possible—to have as little loss as possible in the winnowing, and yet to have it as well winnowed as it may be.

Now, that is what I desire for Christ's church, and what every Christian should desire. We want Christ's church to be as large as possible. God forbid that by any of our winnowing, we would ever cast away one of the precious sons of Zion. When we rebuke sharply, we should be concerned lest the rebuke would fall where it is not needed and bruise and hurt the feelings of any whom God has chosen.

On the other hand, we have no wish to see the church multiplied at the expense of its purity. We do not wish to have a charity so large that it takes in chaff as well as wheat. We want to be charitable enough to use the fan thoroughly to purge God's floor, yet charitable enough to pick up the most shriveled ear of wheat and to preserve it for the Master's sake, who is the Husbandman.

I trust that God will help me to discern between the precious and the vile so that I may say nothing uncharitable that would cut off any of God's people from being part of His true and living and visible church; at the same time, I pray that I may not speak so loosely, and so without God's direction, as to embrace any in the arms of Christian affection whom the Lord has not received in the eternal covenant of His love.

Our text suggests to us three things: first, an inquiry: do we have the Spirit?; second, a caution: if we do not have the Spirit, we are sensual; third, a suspicion: many people separate themselves. Our suspicion concerning them is that notwithstanding their exceptional profession, they are sensual, not having the Spirit; for our text says, *"These be they who separate themselves, sensual, having not the Spirit."*

THE QUESTION

First, then, our text suggests this question: do we have the Spirit? This inquiry is so important that the philosopher may well suspend all his investigations to find an answer to it on his own account. All the great debates of politics, all the most engrossing subjects of human discussion, may well stop today and give us pause to ask ourselves this solemn question: do I have the Spirit? For this question does not deal with any externals of religion, but it deals with religion in its most vital point. He who has the Spirit, although he is wrong in fifty things, being right in this, is saved; he who does not have the Spirit, even if he is ever so orthodox, even if his creed is as correct as Scripture, and if his morals are outwardly as pure as the law, is still unsaved. He is destitute of the essential part of salvation—the Spirit of God dwelling in him.

To help us answer this question, I will try to set forth the effects of the Spirit in our hearts by using several scriptural metaphors. To the question, "Do I have the Spirit?" I reply, "What is the operation of the Spirit? How am I to discern it?" Now the Spirit operates in various ways, all of them mysterious and supernatural, all of them bearing the real marks of His own power, and having certain signs following whereby they may be discovered and recognized.

The Spirit Is like the Wind

The first work of the Spirit in the heart is a work during which the Spirit is compared to the wind. You remember that, when our Savior spoke to Nicodemus, He represented the first work of the Spirit in the heart as being like the wind, which *"blows where it wishes"* (John 3:8 NKJV). Jesus said, *"So is everyone who is born of the Spirit"* (v. 8 NKJV).

Now you know that the wind is a most mysterious thing; and although certain definitions of it pretend to be explanations of the phenomenon, they certainly leave unanswered the great questions of how the wind blows, what the cause of its blowing in a certain direction is, and where it was before. The breath within us, the wind outside us, and all motions of air, are mysterious to us. And the renewing work of the Spirit in the heart is exceedingly mysterious.

It is possible that at this moment the Spirit of God may be breathing into someone who is reading these words, yet it would be blasphemous if anyone would ask, "Which way did the Spirit go from God to that person's heart? How did He enter there?"

It would be foolish for a person who is under the operation of the Spirit to ask how He operates. You do not know where thunder is stored; you do not know where the clouds are balanced; neither can you know how the Spirit goes forth from the Most High and enters into the heart of man.

It may be that, during a sermon, two men are listening to the same truth. One listens as attentively as the other and remembers as much of what he heard as the other man remembers. The other man is moved to tears or filled with solemn thoughts. But the one who was equally attentive sees nothing in the sermon, except, perhaps, certain important truths well presented. As for the other, his heart is broken within him, and his soul is melted.

How is it that the same truth has an effect upon the one and not upon his fellowman? Because the mysterious Spirit of the living God goes with the truth to one heart and not to the other. The one feels only the force of truth, and that may be strong enough to make him tremble, like Felix (see Acts 24); but the other feels the Spirit going with the truth, and that renews and regenerates the man, and causes him to pass into that gracious condition called salvation.

This change takes place instantaneously. It is as miraculous a change as any miracle of which we read in Scripture. It is supremely supernatural. It may be mimicked, but no imitation of it can be true and real. Men may pretend to be regenerated, but without the Spirit, they cannot be. It is a change so marvelous that the highest attempts of man can never reach it. We may reason as long as we please, but we cannot reason ourselves into regeneration. We may meditate until our hairs are gray with study, but we cannot meditate ourselves into the new birth. That is worked in us by the sovereign will of God alone.

> The Spirit, like some heavenly wind,
> Blows on the sons of flesh,
> Inspires us with a heavenly mind,
> And forms the man afresh.

But ask the man how, and he cannot tell you. Ask him when, and he may recognize the time, but as to the manner thereof, he knows no more of it than you do. It is a mystery to him.

You remember the story of the valley of vision. Ezekiel saw dry bones lying scattered here and there in the open valley. The command came to Ezekiel to prophecy to the bones, telling them what God had said—that He would breathe life into them again, and they would live and know that He was the Lord. Ezekiel prophesied, *"and the bones came together, bone to his bone...and the flesh came up upon them"* (Ezek. 37:7–8), but as yet they did not live. Then God said to Ezekiel,

Prophesy unto the wind, prophesy, son of man,
and say to the wind, Thus saith the Lord GOD;
Come from the four winds, O breath, and
breathe upon these slain, that they may live.

(Ezek. 37:9)

They looked as though they were alive. They had flesh and blood, and eyes, hands, and feet, but when Ezekiel spoke the second time, there was a mysterious something given that men call life. It was given in an inexplicable way, like the blowing of the wind.

It is just like that today. Unconverted and ungodly people may be very moral and outstanding individuals, but they are like the dry bones that are put together and clothed with flesh and blood. To make them live spiritually, they need the divine inspiration from the breath of the Almighty, the divine *pneuma,* the divine Spirit. If the divine wind would blow on them, then they would live.

My reader, have you ever had any supernatural influence on your heart? If not, my words may seem to be harsh to you, but I am faithful. If you have never had more than nature in your heart, you are *"in the gall of bitterness, and in the bond of iniquity"* (Acts 8:23). Do not scoff at that statement. It is as true as the Bible, for it was taken from the Bible. Here is the proof: *"Except a man be born again* [from above], *he cannot see the kingdom of God"* (John 3:3). *"Except a man be born of water and of the Spirit, he cannot enter into the kingdom of God"* (v. 5).

What do you say to that? It is in vain for you to talk of making yourself be born again. You cannot be born again except by the Spirit, and you will perish unless you are. You see, then, the first effect of the

Spirit, and by that you may answer the question, Do you have the Spirit?

THE SPIRIT IS LIKE FIRE

Second, the Spirit in the Word of God is often compared to fire. After the Spirit, like the wind, has made the dead sinner live, then comes the Spirit like fire. Now, fire has a searching and tormenting power. It is purifying, but it purifies by a terrible process. After the Holy Spirit has given us the life of Christ, immediately a burning begins in our hearts. The Lord searches and tries our minds, and lights a candle within our spirits that reveals the wickedness of our nature and the loathsomeness of our iniquities. My friend, do you know anything about that fire in your heart? For if not, you have not yet received the Spirit.

To explain what I mean, let me tell something of my own experience, by way of illustrating the fiery effects of the Spirit. I lived carelessly and thoughtlessly. I could indulge in sin as well as others, and did do so. Sometimes my conscience pricked me, but not enough to make me cease from vice. I could indulge in transgression, and I could love it—not as much as others loved it because my early training would not let me do that, but still enough to prove that my heart was debased and corrupt.

One time, something more than conscience pricked me. I did not know then what it was. I was like Samuel, when the Lord called him (see 1 Samuel 3:3–7); I heard the voice, but I did not know from where it came. A stirring began in my heart, and I began to feel that in the sight of God I was a lost, ruined, and condemned sinner. I could not shake off that conviction.

Do what I might, it followed me. If I sought to amuse my mind and distract it from serious thoughts, it was of no use. I was obliged still to carry about with me a heavy burden on my back. I went to my bed, and there I dreamed about hell, and about *"the wrath to come"* (Matt. 3:7). I woke up, and this dreary nightmare, this incubus, still brooded on me. What could I do?

First, I renounced one vicious habit, then another. That did not help. All my efforts were like pulling one firebrand from a flame that fed itself with blazing forests. Do what I might, my conscience found no rest. I went to the house of God to hear the Gospel, but there was no Gospel for me. The fire burned all the more fiercely, and the very breath of the Gospel seemed to fan the flame.

I went to my room to pray. The heavens were like brass, and the windows of the sky were barred against me. I could get no answer. The fire burned more vehemently. Then I thought, "I will not always be alive. I wish to God that I had never been born!" But I dared not die, for I would be in hell when I was dead; but I dared not live, for life had become intolerable. Still the fire blazed vehemently, until at last I came to this resolve: if there is salvation in Christ, I will have it. I have nothing of my own in which to trust. I do this hour, O God, renounce my sin, and renounce my own righteousness, too.

The fire blazed again and burned up all my good works, yes, and my sins with them. And then I saw that all this burning was to bring me to Christ. Oh, the joy and gladness of my heart, when Jesus came and sprinkled water on the flame, and said, "I have bought you with My blood. Put your trust in Me. I will do for you what you cannot do for yourself. I will take your sins away. I will clothe you with a spotless robe of righteousness. I will guide you all your journey through, and land you at last in heaven."

My dear reader, do you know anything about the Spirit of burning? For, if not, again I say—I am not harsh, but I am telling the truth—if you have never felt this, you do not know the Spirit.

The Spirit Is like Oil

To proceed a little further, when the Spirit has thus quickened the soul and convinced it of sin, then we can use the simile of oil to understand the Spirit's work. In the Scriptures, the Holy Spirit is frequently compared to oil. *"Thou anointest my head with oil; my cup runneth over"* (Ps. 23:5). Oh, friends, though the beginning of the Spirit is by fire, it does not end there. We may be first of all convinced and brought to Christ by misery, but when we get to Christ, there is no misery in Him; our sorrows result from not getting close enough to Him.

The Holy Spirit comes, like the good Samaritan, and pours in the oil and the wine. (See Luke 10:30–35.) And, oh, what oil it is with which He anoints our heads, and with which He heals our wounds! How soothing the ointment that He gently applies to our bruises! How blessed the salve with which He anoints our eyes! How heavenly the balm with which He binds up our sores, wounds, and bruises, and makes us whole. He sets our feet upon a rock, and establishes our goings (Ps. 40:2).

The Spirit, after He has convinced, begins to comfort, and you who have felt the comforting power of the Holy Spirit will bear witness that there is no comforter like the Paraclete. Oh, bring the music, singing voices, and the sound of harps to this place. They are medicine to the one who has a heavy heart. Bring me the enchantments of the magic world, and all the enjoyments of its pleasures. They only torment the soul and prick it with many thorns. But, oh, Spirit of the living God, when You blow upon the heart, there is not a wave of that tempestuous sea that does not sleep forever when You bid it to be still. Not one single breath of the proud hurricane and tempest does not cease to howl and does not lie still when You say to it, "Peace be unto you; your sins are forgiven."

Do you know the workings of the Spirit that are like oil? Have you felt Him at work in your spirit, comforting you, anointing your head, making you glad, and causing you to rejoice? There are many people who have never felt this joy. They hope they are religious, but their religion never makes them happy.

Scores of people profess to be Christians who have just enough religion to make them miserable. Let them be afraid that they have any religion at all, for religion makes people happy. When it has its full sway with man, it makes him glad. It may begin in agony, but it does not end there. Say, have you ever had your heart leap for joy? Have your lips ever warbled songs of ecstatic praise? Do your eyes ever flash with the fire of joy? If these things have not happened to you, I fear that you are still without God and without Christ; for where the Spirit comes, His fruits are joy in the Spirit, peace, love, confidence, and assurance forever.

The Spirit Is like Water

Bear with me once more. I want to make one more comparison of the Spirit, and by that also you will be able to ascertain whether you are under His operation. When the Spirit has acted like wind, fire, and oil, He then acts like water. We are told that we are *"born of water and of the Spirit"* (John 3:5). Now I do not think you are foolish enough to need me to say that no water, either of immersion or of sprinkling, can in the least degree operate in the salvation of a soul.

There may be some few poor creatures, whose heads were put on their shoulders the wrong way, who still believe that a few drops of water from a priest's hands can regenerate souls. There may be a few, but I hope that their race will soon die out. We trust that the day will come when all those gentleman will have no *"other gospel"* (Gal. 1:6) to preach. We desire that the terrible stain upon the Protestant Church, called Puseyism,* will be cut out like a cancer and torn out by its very roots. The sooner we get rid of that doctrine the better. Whenever we hear of any of them seceding to Catholicism, we say, "Let them go."

But when the Holy Spirit comes into the heart, He comes like water. That is to say, He comes to purify the soul. He who today lives as wickedly as he did before his pretended conversion is a hypocrite and a liar. He who this day loves sin and lives in it

---

* A religious movement among Anglican clergy at Oxford University in the 1830s. Named after Edward Bouverie Pusey, a professor of Hebrew at Oxford, Puseyism revived certain Roman Catholic doctrines and rituals within the Church of England.

just as he was prone to do before, let him know that the truth is not in him, but that he has received the strong delusion to believe a lie.

God's people are a holy people. God's Spirit works by love and purifies the soul. Once His Spirit comes into our hearts, it will have no rest until it has turned every sin out. God's Holy Spirit and man's sin cannot live together peaceably. They may both be in the same heart, but they cannot both reign there.

Neither can they both be quiet there, for *"the flesh lusts against the Spirit, and the Spirit against the flesh"* (Gal. 5:17 NKJV). They cannot rest, but there will be a perpetual warring in the soul, so that the Christian will have to cry, *"O wretched man that I am! who shall deliver me from the body of this death?"* (Rom. 7:24). But in due time, the Spirit will drive out all sin and will present us blameless before the throne of His Majesty with exceedingly great joy.

Now, my friend, answer this question for yourself and not for any other. Have you received the Holy Spirit? Answer me, even if it is with a scoff. Answer me, even if you sneer and say, "I know nothing of your enthusiastic rhetoric." If that is so, friend, then say, "No." It may be that you do not care to reply at all. I beseech you, do not put away my entreaty. Answer, yes or no. Have you received the Spirit?

"Sir, no man can find fault with my character. I believe I will enter heaven through my own virtues." That is not the question, beloved. Have you received the Spirit? All that you say you may have done, if you have left the other undone and have not received the Spirit, will go ill with you in the end.

Have you had a supernatural operation upon your own heart? Have you been made a *"new creature"* (2 Cor. 5:17) in Christ Jesus? If not, depend on it, because God's Word is true: you are out of Christ. Dying as you are, you will be shut out of heaven, no matter who you are or what you have accomplished in this life.

THE CAUTION

Thus I have tried to help you to answer the first question: have you received the Holy Spirit? This brings me to the caution. He who has not received the Spirit is said to be *"sensual."* Oh, what a gulf there is between the least Christian and the greatest moralist! What a wide distinction there is between the greatest professor of faith who is destitute of grace, and the least of God's believers who has grace in his heart. As great a difference as there is between light and darkness, between death and life, between heaven and hell, is there between a saint and a sinner. Mark what the text says, in no very polite phrase, that if we do not have the Spirit, we are sensual.

"Sensual!" exclaims one. "Well, I am not a converted man—I don't pretend to be—but I am not sensual!" Well, friend, it is very likely that you are not—not in the common understanding of the term *sensual*. But understand that this word, in the Greek, really means what the comparable English word would mean if we had a word such as *soulish*. We do not have such a word, but we need one.

There is a great distinction between mere animals and men, because men have a soul, and animals do not. There is another distinction between mere men and converted men. Converted men have the Spirit, but unconverted men do not. They are soulish men—not spiritual men. They have progressed no further than mere nature and have no inheritance in the spiritual kingdom of grace. It is strange that *soulish* and *sensual* should, after all, mean the same!

Friend, if you do not have the Spirit, then you are nothing better—no matter who you are or what you may be—than the fall of Adam left you. That is to say, you are a fallen creature, having only the capacity to live here in sin and to live forever in torment. But you do not have the capacity to live in heaven at all, for you have no spirit; therefore, you are unable to know or enjoy spiritual things. And mark you, a man may be in this state and be a sensual man, yet he may have all the virtues that could grace a Christian. But even with all these, if he does not have the Spirit, he has gone not an inch farther than where Adam's fall left him—that is, condemned and under the curse. He may attend to religion with all his might—he may take the sacrament, be baptized, and be the most devout professor—but if he does not have the Spirit, then he has not moved a solitary inch from where he was. He is still a lost soul bound by iniquity.

In addition, he may pick up religious phrases until he can talk very glibly about religion. He may read biographies until he seems to be a well-instructed child of God. He may be able to write an article about the deep experience of a believer, but if this experience is not his own, if he has not received it by the Spirit of the living God, he is still nothing more than a carnal man. Heaven is to him a place to which there is no entrance.

Further, he might go so far as to become a minister of the Gospel, and a successful minister, too. God may bless the words that he preaches to the salvation of sinners, but unless he has received the Spirit, even if he is as eloquent as Apollos and as earnest as Paul, he is nothing more than a mere soulish man, without the capacity for spiritual things. To crown all, he might even have the power of working miracles, as Judas had. He might even be received into the church as a believer, as was Simon the Sorcerer. (See Acts 8:9–24.)

After all that, though he had cast out devils, though he had healed the sick, though he had worked miracles, he might have the gates of heaven shut in his face, if he had not received the Spirit. For this is the essential thing, without which all others are in vain: the reception of the Spirit of the living God.

It is a searching truth, is it not, my friends? Do not run away from it. If I am preaching to you falsehood, reject it; but if this is a truth that I can substantiate by Scripture, I beseech you, do not rest until you have answered this question: do you have the Holy Spirit living, dwelling, and working in your heart?

THE SUSPICION

This brings me, in the third place, to the suspicion. How remarkable that "separation" should be the opposite of having the Spirit. I hear a gentleman saying, "Oh, I like to hear you preach smartly and sharply. I am persuaded, sir, that there are a great many people in the church who ought not to be there. Therefore, because there is such a corrupt mixture in the church, I have determined not to join anywhere at all. I do not think that the church of Christ nowadays is at all pure enough to cause me to join with it.

"At least, sir, I did join a church once, but I made such a great deal of noise in it that they were very glad when I went away. And now I am just like David's men. I am one who is in debt and discontented. I go round to hear all new preachers who arise. I have heard you now these three months. I intend to go and hear someone else in a very little time if you do not say something to flatter me. But I am quite sure that I am one of God's special elect. I don't join any church because a church is not good enough for me. I don't become a member of any denomination, because they are all wrong, every one of them."

Listen, brother. I have something to tell you that will not please you. *These be they who separate themselves, sensual, having not the Spirit.* I hope you enjoy the text because it certainly applies to you, above every man in the world. *These be they who separate themselves, sensual, having not the Spirit.*

When I read this verse over, I thought to myself, there are some who would say, "Well, *you* are a dissenter. How do you reconcile this fact with the text, *These be they who separate themselves*? You are separated from the Church of England."

Ah, my friends, a man may be separated from the Church of England and be all the better for it, but the separation intended here is a separation from the one universal church of Christ. The Church of England was not known in Jude's day, so the apostle could not have been referring to it.

"These be they who separate themselves"—that is, from the church of Christ, from the great universal body of the elect. Moreover, let us just say one thing. We did not separate ourselves: we were turned out. Dissenters did not separate themselves from the Church of England, from the Episcopal Church. When the Act of Uniformity was passed, they were turned out of their pulpits. Our forefathers were as sound churchmen as any in the world, but they could not take in all the errors of the Prayer Book, and they were, therefore, hounded to their graves by the intolerance of the conforming professors. So they did not separate themselves.

Moreover, we do not separate ourselves. There is not a Christian beneath the scope of God's heaven from whom I am separated. At the Lord's Table I always invite all churches to come and sit down and commune with us. If anyone were to tell me that I am separated from the Episcopalians, the Presbyterians, or the Methodists, I would tell him that he does not know me, for I love them with a pure heart fervently, and I am not separated from them. I may hold different views than they do, and, in that point, truly I may be said to be separated, but I am not separated from them in my heart. I will work with them—I will work with them heartily. Even though my Church of England brother sends me a summons, as he has done, to pay a church rate* that I cannot in conscience pay, I will love him still. If he comes to claim my chairs and tables for payment, it does not

---

* Abolished in 1868, this local property tax was levied by the Church of England for the upkeep of Anglican parish churches. Separatists, or Nonconformists, protested having to pay this tax.

matter—I will love him still. And if there is a school for poor children or anything else for which I can work with him to promote the glory of God, therein will I unite with him with all my heart.

I think this bears rather hard on our friends— the Strict Communion Baptists. I would not want to say anything hard against them, for they are about the best people in the world, but they really do separate themselves from the great body of Christ's people. The Spirit of the living God will not let them do this really, but they do it professedly. They separate themselves from the great universal church. They say they will not commune with it. If anyone comes to the Lord's Table who has not been baptized, they turn him away.

They separate, certainly. I do not believe it is a willful schism that makes them act this way; but, at the same time, I think the *"old man"* (Eph. 4:22) within has some hand in it. Oh, how my heart loves the doctrine of the one church. The nearer I get to my Master in prayer and communion, the closer I am knit to all His disciples. The more I see of my own errors and failings, the more ready I am to deal gently with those whom I believe to be erring. The pulse of Christ's body is communion, and woe to the church that seeks to cure the ills of Christ's body by stopping its pulse. I think it is a sin to refuse to commune with anyone who is a member of the church of our Lord Jesus Christ.

I desire to preach the unity of Christ's church. I have sought to use the fan to blow away the chaff. I have said that no man belongs to Christ's church unless he has the Spirit; but, if he has the Spirit, woe to the man who separates himself from him. Oh, I should think myself grossly at fault if, coming from the pulpit, I would meet a truly converted child of God who called himself a Primitive Methodist or a Wesleyan or a churchman or an Independent, and I should say, "No, sir, you do not agree with me on certain points. I believe you are a child of God, but I will have nothing to do with you." I should then think that this text would bear very hard on me. *"These be they who separate themselves, sensual, having not the Spirit."* But would we do so, beloved?

No, we would give them both our hands and say, "Godspeed you on your journey to heaven. As long as you have the Spirit within you, we are one family, and we will not be separated from one another."

May God grant that the day will come when every wall of separation will be beaten down! See how to this day we are separate. You will find Episcopalians who hate that ugly word *dissent*. It is enough for them that a Dissenter has done something; they will not do it then, even if it is something good! Furthermore, there are some to be found in the Church of England who not only hate dissenters, but also hate one another in the bargain. Men are to be found who cannot let brother ministers of their own church preach in their parish. What an anachronism such men are! They would seem to have been sent into the world in our time purely by mistake. Their proper era would have been the time of the Dark Ages. If they had lived then, what fine Bonners[*] they would have made! What splendid fellows

---

[*] Edmund Bonner [c. 1500–1569], Bishop of London, was characterized by John Foxe, his contemporary, as a monster who burned Protestants at the stake during the reign of Mary I.

they would have been to have helped to poke the fire in Smithfield.* But they are quite out-of-date in these times, and I look upon such curious clergymen in the same way that I do upon the dodo—as an extraordinary animal whose race is extinct. Well, you may look and look and wonder. It will not be long, I trust, before the Church of England will love itself, and all who love the Lord Jesus will be ready to preach in each other's pulpits, preaching the same truth, holding the same faith, and mightily contending for it. Then will the world "see how these Christians love one another." (See John 13:35.) Then will it be known in heaven that Christ's kingdom has come, and that His will is about to be done on earth as it is in heaven.

My friend, do you belong to the church? For outside of the church, there is no salvation. But mark what the church is. It is not Episcopalian, Baptist, or Presbyterian. The church is a company of people who have received the Holy Spirit. If you cannot say you have the Spirit, go your way and tremble. Go your way and think of your lost condition. May Jesus by His Spirit so bless you that you may be led to renounce with grief your works and ways, fly to Him who died upon the cross, and find a shelter there from the wrath of God.

I may have said some rough things in this message, but I am not given much to cutting corners or diluting the Gospel, and I do not suppose I will begin to learn that art now. If the thing is untrue, it is for

---

* John Lambert was chained and burned at the stake in Smithfield, England, in 1537, after being suspected of having converted to Protestantism.

you to reject. If it is true, reject at your own peril what God stamps with His divine authority. May the blessings of the Father, the Son, and the Holy Spirit rest upon the one church of Israel's one Jehovah. Amen and Amen.